The
RAINY DAY
BOOK

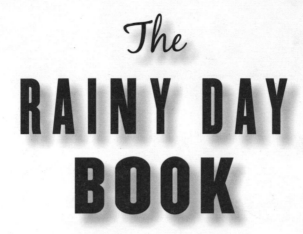

EDITED BY HELEN BROOKS

guardianbooks

Published by Guardian Books 2009

2 4 6 8 10 9 7 5 3 1

First published in Great Britain in 2009 by
Guardian Books
Kings Place, 90 York Way
London N1 9GU

www.guardianbooks.co.uk

A CIP catalogue record for this book
is available from the British Library

ISBN 978-0-85265-139-1
Typeset by www.carrstudio.co.uk

Printed and bound in Great Britain by Clays Ltd, St Ives PLC

The
RAINY DAY
BOOK

CONTENTS

Introduction

EDITING the Family section of the *Guardian* has been a glorious education. Over the years, since its launch issue in September 2005 I have learned to make elderflower cordial, ginger beer and ice cream with salt; I now know how and when to plant garlic and sunflowers, and have become an expert in pharology and phenology.

I have learned how to make gooey slime and wormy farms; I've made a flicker book and a feather pen. I've created candles and an audio diary, a marble run and a time capsule. On occasions my two young sons have joined me in these activities – but I've enjoyed doing them by myself as well.

All these little activities were featured in our 'If I Had the Time' section, on the back page of Family. The idea behind it was to offer simple, uplifting ideas for lovely things to do as a family, which would involve spending time together without spending enormous sums of money.

The title of the feature acknowledged that lives are busy, and there's not always enough time to devote to home and family. But our aspiration was to offer ideas so inspiring, ingenious and effortless (sometimes at least) that you would make the time.

We didn't want it to be a purely listings guide, though we have always tried to include interesting and off-beat events around the country. What we wanted predominantly was to come up with creative, home-grown ideas, that could be done at or near home, with the minimum of expense and limited know-how. Oh, and they had to be beautifully written too, so even if you didn't find the time to do them, you could take pleasure in reading about them.

Sometimes they have been sweet reminders of simple pleasures that may get forgotten in the hurly burly of our high-stress urban existence – the joy of walking through bluebells or tiptoeing around snowdrops; look at the stars, swim in the open air, walk by a river. Learn how to make stones bounce over water with Ian Sansom's guide to the art of stone skimming, and hold a bubble competition, inspired by Vincent Reid.

On a personal note, I will always be thankful to Louisa Young who urged readers to let their children make dinner for them; I now have a 13-year-old son who is passionate about cooking and regularly caters for the whole family, friends and relations. What a result!

In more recent times, as Family has been tweaked and improved and finessed, 'If I Had the Time' has evolved into 'Weekend Planner', but the ingenuity of our contributors continues to astonish and amaze. How does Ian Sansom know so much? Good Lord, his children must be brainy! And how on earth does Melissa Viguier dream up those extraordinary craft projects?

And now many of their wonderful ideas have been collected in this lovely book. So the great thing is, that even if you and your children (or your mother-in-law, or your godson, or your second cousin removed) don't have time right now to learn how to make a cloud, to predict the weather or learn the art of semaphore signals, you now have this perfect little collection always to hand for an idle moment one quiet, rainy – or sunny – weekend.

SALLY WEALE

EDITOR, FAMILY

Rainy days

Things to make and do indoors

Make your own flicker book

✳

A flicker book is basically a pocket-size film, conjured up by inventive Victorians, and it is a brilliant way of telling a story in pictures. The principle is amazingly simple: you make a small book (about the size of a box of matches), and draw an image on each page. The images make a sequence, so when you flick the pages quickly the images spring to life.

We began one wet, windy afternoon in January, with just one sheet of A4 paper (times are hard) which we cut into three long strips, then each of these was cut into nine, so we ended up with 27 little rectangles. Shuffled and made into a tidy pile then stapled together along one of the short edges, they made a small book. The pages need to be decorated with a sequence of events – we were inspired by a trip to a local castle, so with sharpened pencils we began drawing a mountain on page one. On page two, we drew the same image but with a man and an axe next to it. On page three, the man began breaking the mountain into small rocks. And so on until the same man built a tower out of the rocks, then four more and turned them into a castle, with a drawbridge. Just as he raised the flag, who should arrive but an attacking army – which knocked the castle down.

If you just have five minutes and want to dip a toe in the world of flicker books there is an easier way. You just need a pad of Post-it notes, and you can draw a ball bouncing up and down, or a bird taking off and flying.

MELISSA VIGUIER

Go back to basics with balsa

✳

Woodwork with pre-schoolers might not be your idea of fun, or a child-safe activity; but it has proved to be surprisingly successful in our home. We only use balsa wood (which is so soft you could probably cut it with scissors).

Our first project consisted just of sawing and sandpapering. We began by clamping the balsa wood in a vice to the table. Then, primed with junior hacksaws, the fun began. I helped steady the wood as they sawed back and forth, then we smoothed it off with sandpaper.

Another five sessions like this resulted in enough pieces of wood to make a box, which we assembled with wood glue and tiny pin nails. This great achievement unleashed a flurry of ideas of things the box could be turned into – a trolley, a buggy, a car, aeroplane – and we finally settled on a rowing boat. So I carefully pierced two holes in the two long sides of the box, and we fashioned some oars to go through the holes.

MELISSA VIGUIER

Share the pleasure of knitting

✳

SHARING our childhood pleasures with our own children can be a risky business, because it doesn't necessarily follow that they'll enjoy the same things as us. I'm glad I took the chance with knitting though. A winter can't pass by without me knitting some form of garment or present, and this year I've roped in my oldest child too.

We began with thick wooden knitting needles, and chunky wool and the 'dual control' method, where we both hold the needles, and knit a few rows, very slowly, just in plain or purl stitch. The objective was to knit a blanket for a toy, and a very small blanket doesn't take long with chunky wool, so this kept enthusiasm high.

To make it rhythmic and easier to understand we made a little rhyme to remember how to make a plain style stitch – it goes like this: 'In through the doorway, run round the house, shut the door, and go next door'.

We plan to keep knitting small square-ish shapes like this, and eventually join them up to make a bigger blanket or hot-water bottle cover.

MELISSA VIGUIER

Become a master printer

✳

KIDS love to do crafty things such as sticking bits of coloured paper on a cereal box and declaring it a monster. But glue is so sticky and it tends to end up in hair. Scissors have a nasty habit of chopping unintended things, such as the rug or the couch. One solution to craft time that pleases everyone is to get printing. Printmaking is not excessively messy and it does get the creative juices flowing. One technique, the monoprint, is perfect for kids.

Find a large sheet of glossy cardboard, such as an old cereal packet. Paint your image on to the shiny, non-absorbent side of the cardboard. Tape a piece of paper to the side of the cardboard so that you can flip it over on top of the printed surface (this makes the actual print by transferring the paint from the cardboard to the paper when you press down hard on it). You can then wipe the cardboard down and do a different print or use other colours to build up your original image.

If this is too easy, you can try drypoint printing. This is where you use a sharp instrument to lightly cut a picture into the cardboard. Next, cover the cardboard with paint or ink, then wipe it all off again. Paint should remain in the lines and grooves that you have made. Cover the cardboard with paper and give the back of the paper a good rub. It might not be what the grown ups do with printing presses and acids, but the results can still be remarkable.

VINCENT REID

Make papier-mâché food

✳

PAPIER-MÂCHÉ is perfect for making props for children's role play. It's very easy to make, fun and cheap, and the results can be strong but light. A good starter project is making pretend food. All you need is a pile of old newspaper, a mixing bowl with about 300ml of water in it, flour and some balloons. Pour the flour into the water, mixing as you go, until it makes a nice gloopy paste. Then tear the paper into strips, approximately 3cm wide and 10cm long.

We started by making apples. First we blew the balloons up to the size of an apple. Then take a strip of paper and dip it into the mixture, then lay it on to the balloon. Repeat until the balloon is entirely covered with three layers of papier-mâché. Leave it for a couple of days to dry, then paint it. We used the same technique to make pears, tomatoes, bananas (with sausage balloons) and carrots.

MELISSA VIGUIER

Turn the bed into a pirate ship

✳

CHILDREN's beds have an annoying habit of being unmade in the morning. What better way to make a bed than to transform it into a pirate ship? Follow these instructions and you can't go wrong.

Name your ship. You can go for modern, such as Whitbread, or classic, such as Dancing Mermaid. Give your crewmates names such as Captain Bligh and Mr Calamity. Take the topsheet and throw it over the headboard. This is your sail. Let your crew know that you are hoisting it. Singing a hoisting song at this juncture is optional but can help to get the crew into the mood.

Make sure that all the crew members are on the bed, thereby ensuring that they are not eaten by sharks. Do not forget to remind them of the shark threat at regular intervals. After a good deal of hauling ropes, holding the tiller and avoiding angry whales, it is time to arrive at the islands.

In the past, we have arrived at islands where we make pirate hats, among other things. The most regularly visited island in our house is the kitchen. Make the crew 'row' to your destination in an imagined longboat – synchronise their rowing strokes so that oars don't get tangled.

In the kitchen, bowls, spoons, cereal and fruit are loaded on to a tray, placed in the longboat and taken back to the main ship. It is now time for the pirates' breakfast. At this time the crew will be having so much fun that you can duck off and read the paper. You can make the bed when the kids are out of the way.

VINCENT REID

Make a portrait of someone

※

WE are used to seeing photos of ourselves and our reflection in the mirror, but seeing a shadow drawing of your profile is something quite different.

All you need is a poseable lamp, a pencil, rubber and ruler, a piece of A3 card or paper, Blu-Tack and finally someone to draw and a chair or stool for them to sit on. Before setting up the equipment you can make things easier for yourself by drawing a grid in pencil on to the piece of card or paper. Divide into approximately 5cm x 5cm squares.

Place the chair against one corner of a wall, and ask your subject to sit down, with their shoulder touching the wall. Then stick the paper on the wall just next to your subject, and make sure that the shadow from their head and shoulders will fall roughly in the middle of the paper. Now place your lamp angled towards their head, and 2m away from the wall. Switch it on, then trace the shadow profile on to the paper. Afterwards you can fill in the shadow with black paint and there you will have a unique portrait.

MELISSA VIGUIER

Build a scale model of a room

✳

THERE are two really good things about getting new shoes: first the shoes, and second the box. We have a fascination with good strong boxes in our home and shoe boxes definitely fall into this category.

During one slow rainy day recently we decided to turn a shoe box into a scale model of a room in our house. We chose the living room, because it is rectangular (like the shoe box) and full of interesting furniture to make.

We measured the room and the shoe box and decided that the room was just about 13 times longer and wider than the shoe box. Then we set to work measuring the table and chairs, fireplace, windows, door, bookshelves and so on. And all the measurements were divided by 13.

Then, using cereal boxes, food cartons, tape and glue, we made some furniture to scale. The room was painted in realistic magnolia and white using the leftovers from the paint we actually used in the house, and the windows and door were partially cut out (so they could open and shut).

Finally, we chose to leave the lid of the shoe box intact so we could have a giant's view of our living room.

MELISSA VIGUIER

Give a toy a funeral

※

Iget killed four to five times a day, on average. This is not a problem, as my slayer usually magically resurrects me on the condition that I confirm that I was killed fairly.

Why are three- to five-year-old kids so fascinated with death? Freud amusingly suggested in his theory of instincts that at this age children begin to have a death wish. Various religions also have their ideas on what this is all about. To me, it is more likely that kids find death confusing.

How can people suddenly cease to exist? Anything that is mystifying is, of course, stunningly interesting. We once lasted an hour-long car journey without anyone screaming in boredom – all because we were conducting a Q&A session on death rituals for a rapt audience of two preschoolers.

But my son got the shock of his life when he really 'killed' one of his toys. Between racking sobs I was implored to put Captain Bligh back together. The cannonball had hit the toy square on the head. There was no way it was ever going to be the same again. Disaster was quickly averted by Mum's quick thinking: 'Perhaps we could do a pirate's funeral?' For some reason, the idea of a funeral hit the jackpot. Particularly when there was chocolate on offer at the wake. Captain Bligh's life and untimely death were mourned in style and then promptly forgotten. I was being slain again within 24 hours. From my son's perspective, everything was back to normal. Dead people were being resurrected and life could continue as planned.

VINCENT REID

Write on everything

※

I T'S a fact that small children write on walls. I myself once
wrote that my brother was a nit. Then crossed out his name
and put mine, so the parents would think he had done it.
But writing on things is mostly an innocent pleasure if done
right. Like Half-Man Half-Biscuit, we can enjoy writing on
the soles of our slippers, in Biro. School hours can be enjoyed
by painting school soles with Tipp-Ex. Biro also works well on
old jeans. With a chinagraph pencil (available from art shops,
in red, green and white) you can draw all over your mirrors,
windows, windscreens etc. I currently apply my mascara
through portraits of Emily the Strange. Lipstick messages
on mirrors of course have a glamour all of their own. A roll
of lining paper pinned up to cover a vast expanse will let
youngsters think they really are writing on the wall, with
added naughtiness thrill points.

Little cakes, each iced with a letter of the alphabet, make
for educational preschool fun. Make the word, then eat it! It is
also possible with practice to make pancakes in the shape of
initials, or, if greedy, an entire name, letter by letter. Flipping
is an advanced technique – beware.

Best of all (though dependent on the season): grow marrows.
While they're young and tender, use a pin to scratch your
name on one. By the time it is big, your name will be five
times the size, in strong, brown scar tissue.

LOUISA YOUNG

Make a memory box

✳

WITH my two young children there is so much I want to remember, but so little time to organise those memories. That's why I made a memory box. I keep it in the back of my wardrobe. It's just a cardboard box, but is stuffed full of tatty A4 envelopes and cloth bags, each containing the memories of a year. It's easy to make, I just keep an open envelope on a handy shelf, and each time we do something we want to remember, my children and I put a souvenir from the day in the envelope.

Then at the end of the year I just write the date on the envelope and put it in the memory box, safe in the knowledge that, one day, I'll open that special envelope again and it will bring the memories flooding back.

MELISSA VIGUIER

Make a giant picture

※

DRAWING on a giant scale is unbelievably exciting: it always feels a bit daring, and very physical as you move your whole body, not just one hand.

This is not all though – the sheer scale of it makes you feel as if you are inside the picture yourself. We begin by unrolling a roll of wallpaper lining paper down the floor of the hallway, then armed with pens and paint we set to work. My children love to lie on the paper and be drawn around, then they decorate their pictures. On a giant scale anything is possible. We've made a picture of a holiday landscape that we wrapped around the inside of a room, and life-size pictures of animals and machines. You can turn the roll over and reuse it, make it into posters or just pin it up in their gallery bedroom.

MELISSA VIGUIER

Blow giant bubbles

✳

A basic jar of bubble mix will amuse toddlers for hours (or at least until it gets spilled) but, for older kids, you need something more impressive – and that means giant bubbles. Commercial bubble mix is usually too thin for record-breaking bubbles, so you'll want to make your own, using a recipe of roughly 600ml of water to four tablespoons of washing-up liquid to one tablespoon of glycerine (sold in chemists as a cough remedy). Gently mix the liquid, then pour it into a large, shallow-ish tray – a large baking tray is ideal.

For a wand, you can bend wire coat-hangers into circles, or thread drinking straws on string to form rectangles that you dip into the liquid and draw out through the air to form a bubble.

You can also make a circle with your thumb and index finger, then dip it in the liquid and blow gently. Or use both hands to make a larger circle.

To really go for it, fill a paddling pool with the mix, get a child to stand in it, then use a hula hoop to draw out an enormous bubble, completely encasing the child. The world record for the number of children encased in one bubble is 50. It was set at the Science Museum in London in 2007. I think we'll need a bigger pool ...

HELEN DAVIES

Create your own marble run

*

THERE are lots of marble runs you can buy, but it is much more fun to create your own with junk and duct tape. We rummaged through our recycling box for bits and pieces we thought would work well: the long, corner edges of boxes for V-shaped chutes; the tubes from wrapping paper for tunnels; the tops of milk cartons for marbles to plop through, toilet rolls with slits, bent for elbow joints at corners; and a fruit punnet for collecting the marbles at the bottom. We started upstairs at the far end of the landing and worked our way downstairs, securely taping the pieces to the side of the stairs and bannister. I saw the engineer in my nine-year-old son emerge as he thought of increasingly creative ways to use stuff, but his was a spectacular spinning plug-hole effect that he accidentally created with the cut-off top of a squash bottle. Two-and-a-half hours and nine metres later, we rolled our first marble from top to bottom. 'Cool! Wouldn't it be great if we were small enough to slide down it?' he said.

CLAIRE POTTER

Make a time capsule

＊

TIME capsules are fantastic things to discover after many years of being forgotten. They can be very personal, and allow someone to see what they were interested in at a specific point in their lives.

Alternatively, they can commemorate an event, such as a birthday. Or they can be used as an index of what was going on in the world politically. Our recent time capsule contained a copy of the *Guardian*, together with drawings by the kids, photos of the family and a list of the interests and hobbies of all family members. All these items managed to fit into a shoe box. Contrary to common belief, a time capsule does not need to be buried.

Good locations to keep a time capsule include the top of a wardrobe, under a bed or at the back of a cupboard. Anywhere will do, so long as it won't be disturbed and it will not be left behind should you move house.

The real buzz is the knowledge that you will discover it at a later date, and before you open it, you will wonder what is inside. Adults should be prepared not to laugh when a five-year-old opens their time capsule and reminisces about how everything was just so different when they were four.

When you think about it, they are completely right.

VINCENT REID

Make a mask

✳

MY five-year-old twins have learnt to hide. Until recently, they stood in front of me, hands over their eyes, and shouted, 'Bet you can't see us!' But now they've reached the sofa-shifting stage, knowing that to be undetected they have to conceal all their body behind large pieces of furniture.

Until, that is, they came across *The Thief Lord*, the film based on Cornelia Funke's wonderful novel about a boy who dons a mask to become a modern-day Robin Hood in the back alleyways of Venice.

The Thief Lord's mask, although only covering half his handsome young face, manages to disguise him completely. So the kids are convinced they can work the same trick on me.

They made their masks from nothing more than an empty cereal packet, a bottle of black paint, and two rubber bands. Under instruction from their big sister (I'm not a sticking-and-gluing type of mother), they cut out the shape of the Thief Lord's simple beaked mask and painted it black, just like in the film. Elastic bands were attached through a hole at each side and hooked behind their ears. Then they stood right in front of me and shouted, 'Bet you can't see us!' Of course, I pretended I couldn't.

At least they're no longer shifting the sofa.

DEA BIRKETT

The Thief Lord (cert PG), is available to buy on DVD, see www.amazon. co.uk

Make a pinhole camera

※

IT'S inspiring to think that while we are surrounded by technology in our daily lives, a cardboard tube with a tiny hole in it is all you really need to capture a moment in time. The pinhole camera or *camera obscura* – Latin for dark chamber – can be made out of almost any item, making it one of the most affordable and traditional methods for taking pictures.

To make a simple pinhole: find an empty cardboard tube with a lid and metal bottom. Draw a line round the outside of the tube with a marker pen, a couple of inches up from the bottom, then cut along it so the tube is in two pieces.

Make a tiny hole in the centre of the metal bottom, using a pin.

Stick a piece of white tissue paper inside the lid then put it on to the shorter tube. Then tape the longer tube to the shorter one. Tape a piece of aluminium foil round the outside of the entire tube making sure there are no gaps for light to sneak in. On a bright day go outside and hold the tube up to one eye. The lid inside the tube will act as a screen, showing you upside down pictures.

This camera won't take a photograph but is a satisfying, hands-on introduction to pinhole and if it converts you from your digital screen there are charming vintage pinholes and affordable do-it-yourself kits available on the internet and in many museum gift shops.

LYDIA FULTON

Record an audio diary

✳

CHILDREN change and grow very fast and a day-in-our-life audio diary is a fascinating way to appreciate this. We first did this on a day's boating when our son was a baby. I assumed the role of narrator and interviewer, and used a simple hand-held Dictaphone. I began recording snippets of the day as we woke up in the morning, and you can hear my son eating breakfast and gurgling as I ask him if he likes porridge. Then there is the sound of clicking seatbelts in the car, followed by traffic noises as we drive to the boat. I recorded the sounds of us getting in the boat and setting sail. Then you can hear the lapping of water and the rest of us chatting about the birds we can see and the jellyfish floating past.

Finally, the day was rounded off by the sounds of dinner, and bath time and bedtime in the evening. In all, I recorded about one hour of the day and it serves as a very funny reminder of life four years ago, and how we all were at the time.

We've repeated the diary once a year since, and now have a mini archive that will no doubt give us pleasure for years to come.

MELISSA VIGUIER

Create a family picture tree

※

RATHER than tracing your roots, trace your cleft chin, thin lips or Roman nose through a family picture tree. To assist my six-year-old son with a school project, we recently drew out a family tree. The result was a flat sketch with names and dates that meant little to him. To add some interest we decided to create a picture tree: a family tree with the addition of baby photos.

The call went out to grandparents to dust off the albums and pull out the baby pictures. Several hours were then lost in a reminiscent haze as everyone pored over the results.

Baby photographs of family born in the 1940s we managed, but beyond that it proved difficult. I have only one photograph of my grandparents: on their wedding day, looking startled in their Sunday best.

To assemble your tree, start with a pencil sketch on a piece of card (A2 or larger) and mark out positions for the pictures. We restricted our tree to immediate family, leaving out cousins. To preserve the photos, use a scanner to make copies, which you can then cut out. Then, starting with the oldest generation, work across the top, jumping down a step with each generation so that the youngest end up somewhere near the bottom/middle of the card. PVA or spray-mount glue works best to fix the photos in place.

The children had fun guessing who the babies were, and immediately drew out similarities in looks, in one case confusing their Auntie Suzanne with a school-day photograph of their granny.

For more information on tracing your family history, a good place to start is www.familyrecords.gov.uk. This site has a useful beginner's guide and links to other websites.

JOANN LEEDING

Record your family history

✳

WHEN I was a child I discovered a box of old letters in the loft. They were from my Great-aunt Wynne to her fiancé during the second world war, and they were absolutely captivating to read. But what would have made them even more valuable is if there had been any recordings of my great-aunt.

There is something irresistible about hearing a good tale from another era, so I have decided to make an oral-history archive of and for my family. I built up a list of the oldest and wisest family members and set my parents the task of digging out any old photos or objects that might trigger memories. I briefed the kids on the how and why of oral history and they became enthusiastic assistants. We came up with some questions: where and when they were born; what their childhood was like; if they ever fell in love; the most exciting thing they ever did; what they did for a job, what shaped their life and, finally, what they think the future will be like.

As we work our way round the relatives, we are slowly creating a snapshot of who our family really is – what they believe in and are passionate about – not just their statistics.

The Oral History Society: www.ohs.org.uk

MELISSA VIGUIER

Turn a pebble into art

✳

WALKING on the beach, stones become a pretty important part of the experience. Kick them, aim them, skim them ... or collect them. Some stones are beautiful in themselves, but if you want to do the beautifying yourself, the best stones to look for are the white, slightly porous ones.

You don't have to use paint, though. My son prefers felt pens – easier, more accurate, quicker drying. Stones can take any kind of artistic design – drawings of animals or landscapes, faces, or abstract designs. You can decorate small stones and group them together in a bowl or on a mantelpiece, or use a larger rock as a paperweight or a door stop. If you are using felt pens, it is worth varnishing your stones. We have learned to our cost that if you don't, the pen slowly fades until you are left once again with (almost) pure white stone. Though you could always return it to the beach.

JULIET RIX

Dye T-shirts with onion skins

※

IT's great fun to dye clothes as children get a kick out of making their own unique items of apparel. The easiest way to make a dye is to collect onion skins. These will produce a vibrant yellow colour. You need about 500g of skins, which will make enough dye for three or four T-shirts. First boil your white shirts with some washing powder in five litres of water for 60 minutes and then leave to soak for 24 hours.

Reheat the water until warm and mix in two tablespoons of cream of tartar. This will fix the dye. Leave the T-shirts to soak for 24 hours then rinse.

Boil the onion skins for about an hour in 10 litres of water until the water is dark. Remove the skins and add the T-shirts. Keep the water warm but under boiling point until your T-shirts are dyed to the degree you want. Rinse them a few times before hanging out to dry. To create patterns, roll the material into sausage shapes and tie them tightly with string before putting in the dye. Don't be surprised when these items of clothing become hot favourites with the children.

VINCENT REID

Build a xylophone

✳

WE began with a child's size mini xylophone. In order to extend this to make a giant xylophone, measuring 1.5m, we just scaled up the design. Beginning with the frame, which is roughly A-shaped, we screwed together four pieces of wood – it can be any length; it just needs to be strong and A-shaped.

Then, for the bars, we made 25 all from pine, by just sawing the wood into lengths with our hacksaws. Each bar is 2cm longer than the previous one. Then each bar was drilled at each end (by an adult) using a 6mm drill bit, and all the bars were laid on to the frame with a gap between bars of approximately 5mm.

Finally, the bars are held in place by nails through the holes. It's important that they can move a little to resonate the sound, so don't nail too close. Make sure that the bars aren't touching each other. Knots in the wood, and bends and splits, all affect the sound waves – but are fun to experiment with.

MELISSA VIGUIER

Make an air-powered boat

✳

WE enjoy finding new uses for items that normally get thrown away. One amusing invention is an air-powered boat made from a humble plastic water bottle, with the aid of a party balloon. The vessel doesn't have any moving parts and no tools are required. Instead of throwing your empty bottle (preferably the flat-sided sort with a sports cap) into a recycling bin, use a drawing pin or compass point to make a hole a little larger than a pinhead. It should be towards the top but below the tapered neck.

Then the fun starts. Blow a few puffs into the balloon and, without releasing the air, attach it to the bottle's open cap. Place the bottle, punctured side down, into your pond or bath and watch it go. The air slowly bubbles through the hole, giving just enough thrust to propel the 'boat' gently through the water, often with the accompaniment of a realistic 'phut-phut' sound.

It keeps young children occupied for ages, especially if you encourage them to experiment by adding weight or decorating the sides with card and crayons so it looks the part. Maybe they will get the bottle-boat bug, producing a small fleet of them for racing. Don't forget to impress everyone by stating that the exercise demonstrates Newton's third law of motion: that every action has an opposite and equal reaction.

BOB BARTON

Launch a rocket

✳

IT makes more of a pop than a bang, it's true, but it does fly well ('high enough to be fun' as my son put it). And it only takes five minutes to make.

All you need is a 35mm film canister, a bit of Blu-Tack, and an Alka-Seltzer or fizzy vitamin C tablet. Break the tablet into four and tack a quarter onto the inside of the lid. Fill the canister a quarter full of water.

Being careful to ensure no water touches the tablet, put the lid on the canister and keep upright. Take your mini-rocket outside and, when you are ready for take-off, place the canister upside down on a flat patch of ground and retreat. Wait for it! It takes just long enough for the kids to start thinking it isn't going to work – but (as long as the tablet stays dry) it always does.

For the scientifically minded, what happens is that the water reacts with the tablet to produce carbon dioxide. The gas builds up until the pressure is so great it bursts out, jetting the canister into the air.

JULIET RIX

Make your own pomander ball

✳

Apomander ball is an orange studded with cloves and rolled in spices. Simple but effective, with a delicious aroma. In medieval times they were used to counteract the vile stenches of the age. Children still love to make pomanders as gifts and decorations for Christmas.

Little fingers might need some help to get the cloves in. Use a wooden toothpick or cocktail stick to make holes in the orange skin, then carefully press a clove into each one. The design is up to you, and you can get really artistic, marking out hearts, diamonds, initials and criss-cross patterns. The orange will shrink a bit as it dries, so leave some space between the cloves.

Next, put your studded orange into a plastic bag with some ground cinnamon and maybe nutmeg, and give it a good shake. It comes out looking dusty, so wrap it in tissue paper and leave to dry out in a warm place, such as an airing cupboard, for up to six weeks.

Finally, tie some ribbon around the orange like a parcel, making a loop to hang it up by. If the kids show signs of going into mass production, you can bulk buy the cloves from a health-food store or Asian grocer. Lemons and limes are just as good, and if you miss out rolling them in the spices, you'll have a multicoloured display.

LESLEY CARR

Make a rubber-band ball

＊

MY kids no longer want Sylvanian Families or Heelys. The latest essential toy is a rubber-band ball. It costs nothing and you make it yourself. For months our daughters had taken an unusual interest in the discarded red rubber bands that our postman drops outside the front door with every delivery. So we thought we'd turn them into a ball.

We crumpled up a tissue for the centre of the ball and then started wrapping the bands around it. Once a critical mass of bands was reached the children were amazed to find the ball bounced in a variety of directions. So now the challenge is to collect ever more bands on the run. It's amazing how many postal workers drop. Even the dullest of walks is enlivened by the children spotting another rogue elastic band.

We've even found bands in different cities and added them to the kids' burgeoning balls. Six-year-old Nell likes the colour of the bands, while nine-year-old Lola enjoys the thrill of making her own toy. In fact, we may have started a cult; Lola's friend Maya has also started constructing a band ball.

The future is elastic. Entertain your kids for free and help Royal Mail reduce its rubber-band mountain.

PETE MAY

There's a Hippo in my Cistern by Peter May is published by Collins.

Make seeds into a sci-fi cartoon

✳

'THE Nasty Urchins put up a brave defence, as they marched forward. Packed shoulder to shoulder they waded across the remains of the lawn, crawling over everything in their path to get to the Impatiens frontline ...'

This is an extract from *The Pod Beasts*, a science-fiction cartoon my son and I made based on our experiments in the back garden with seeds and a magnifying glass. Every year we relish the seed-gathering ritual. We cut down the dead plants and, before chucking them on the compost, pour the seeds into an empty film canister, label them, and put them in the shed over winter. This year, however, we decided to have a really good look at those seeds through our magnifying glasses. Close up, these brown wrinkly dots take on a whole new persona: suddenly you see their intricate design and they look almost alien-like, which is where the sci-fi cartoon comes in.

It began with character development. Some of the seeds had knarled 'wicked old man' faces, so they became the Nasty Urchins (Nasturtiums). And others had a smooth, younger-looking texture, now known as the Imps (Impatiens).

Using a photo we had taken through the magnifying glass, we drew the seeds with different expressions: happy, angry, determined, then running, crawling and so on. This gave us a bit of time to develop the plot. Then, taking a sheet of paper, my son drew a box for the title, another next to it for the first scene, and before long we had a 23-scene cartoon.

MELISSA VIGUIER

Make art from everything

✳

OUR kids love cutting stuff up, especially the two-year-old. He's Edward Scissorhands, only with less self-restraint. He chops up all he sees, which is why I am grateful for the supply of free paper that comes through the letterbox. The weekly report from Lidl becomes a pile of colourful scraps. They're like fish scales, somebody says. The glue comes out.

As a family we are scavengers and hoarders of sweet wrappers, bottle tops, scraps of shiny paper, electrical wire and what not. So now the fish gets a shiny belly, some fins, a big eye, teeth. Mama gives up a treasured box, once a pasta packet which has green cellophane on the front – perfect for seaweed.

Some overzealous gluing turns the fish's back into a sludgy mess. No matter. Fresh scales have just arrived, care of our local Lib Dem councillor. Unfortunately, our scale cutter decides to crumple them. Then he turns with glee towards the fish. There's pandemonium as his big sister tries to save it. The fish doesn't stand a chance.

The scissors, meanwhile, have quietly disappeared.

JAMES RUSSELL

How to Turn Your Parents Green by James Russell is published by Tangent Books.

Melt and make candles

※

WE began with the wax remains from some candles, broken into little bits by the kids, and melted down in a saucepan (by the adult), where any debris will sink to the bottom. The saucepan we use is in fact two pans: a large one with water in, and a small one that sits inside with all the old bits of wax in. When the wax melts you can pour off the clean wax, leaving the debris behind in the pan. You have to work quite quickly at this point, so have all the moulds ready prepared. We use three types of mould: whole egg shells (supported in an egg box); a thick lipped glass, or mini jam jar; and those disposable metal cases that you find on individual fruit tarts.

Suspend a birthday candle over the mould (using an outstretched paper clip over the top of your mould to hold it in place) – this will be the new candle wick. Then pour in the melted wax, wait for it to cool, remove the paper clip and the kids can paint the outside of the eggs, or glass.

MELISSA VIGUIER

Play with clay

＊

A bag of modelling clay can be a welcome diversion on occasions such as Christmas when the generations gather together. I'm not talking about the squidgy red gunk beloved of old-fashioned pottery teachers, but a smooth silver clay with fibres embedded so that it doesn't need to be fired at all. It comes in big plastic sacks, which – kept sealed and covered with a damp cloth – will last for a good year.

Just slap a lump of it down in front of each guest and you'd be surprised how the age gaps melt away. It's not the sort of thing most adults get their hands on very often, and for inhibited initiates you can get booklets showing how to make old-fashioned coil pots. But most people soon get the hang of it, and children seem to take to it immediately.

A recent session involving several girls under 12 resulted in a fabulous stud farm of horses, which have since been painted. An anxious friend modelled her ageing father in loving detail and went home feeling much cheerier, while my daughter turned out a portrait of me which I hope owes more to imagination than insight.

It can be useful, too, for children's parties that are getting to the tired and teary stage – just beware of boys firing clay cannonballs.

CLAIRE ARMITSTEAD

Make a button box

✳

WHEN I was a child my nan kept an old button box high on a shelf in the pantry. If we had been good my brother and I were allowed to take the tin down, spill its contents and rummage to our heart's desire.

The button box was magical for a child. To an adult its contents may have looked rather ordinary, consisting mostly of odd buttons, beads and ribbons. However, to us it was like running our hands through a treasure chest, pretending we had found precious stones or real gold. Occasionally we would find gems such as my nan's bobbie pins from the 1920s or my grandad's war ration book.

I'm not sure what happened to the button box after my grandparents passed away. However, the tradition has passed on to my mum who keeps an assortment of buttons and old cloth badges in a wooden box.

I, too, have started a small button box for my daughter to rummage through. It's easy to collect odd buttons, fasteners and ribbons and she seems particularly fascinated with sorting the colours, shapes and textures.

I must try to remember, though, to include a few items of our everyday life for my grandchildren to rummage through one day. It's funny how family history is carried around in old boxes of buttons and odds and ends.

KATHRYN HOULDCROFT

Make a feather pen

✳

WE can never seem to find a pen in our house, but now we have mastered quill pen-making, we will always have plenty.

We began with some large swan feathers, with nice thick stems and no splits or cracks in them. Then, armed with a very sharp pair of scissors, we began working our way through the four basic stages of quill creation:

1. Cut the tip of the feather's stem off at a 45-degree angle.
2. Make a 1.5cm slit up the stem of the feather from the top of the first cut you made. Scoop out any visible membranes.
3. Widen the slit to make it into a scoop shape (enlarging that very first cut you made), but be careful not to cut the scoop deeper than the top half of the stem.
4. Turn the scoop into an elegant nib by trimming it with the scissors. It should be symmetric, and taper to a neat point.

You have to dip the quill in ink every second letter, and every few sentences we have to sharpen the nib a little, but the whole process is great fun. Of course, you can make your own ink too, from the juice of festering ink cap mushrooms, or by mixing some egg white with soot and a little honey.

MELISSA VIGUEIR

Make a kite

✳

O N those crisp days in winter when the sky is bright blue, what could be more fun than taking a kite out? It's even better if you make the kite yourself. Follow these simple instructions and you'll be finished and flying in no time.

You will need:

90cm lengths of dowelling, fine bamboo or garden stakes

A large piece of paper, ideally 100cm x 75cm (try a disposable paper tablecloth)

Paper glue in a liquid, and/or spray-mount

A blob of wood glue

Scotch tape, or better, brightly coloured gaffer tape

Decorative materials and lots of string

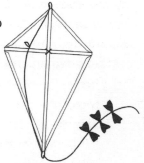

Begin by cutting your sticks into two pieces, one slightly shorter than the other. Make a cross with the sticks, by placing the shorter stick across the longer one about two thirds of the way along its length. Cut little notches at the intersection so that they don't slide about, and fix in position with wood glue and a bit of string binding, which children can help with. Next cut some notches in the four ends of your kite frame, and stretch some string between them to create that well-known diamond shape. Children can help by holding it in the grooves while you tighten it and tie it off. Make a loop at the top and tail end.

It is often easier to decorate your kite before the paper goes on, so cut out a diamond about 3cm bigger than your kite frame, supply paints and crayons, and stand well back as the little ones get to work. When everything is dry, fold and glue carefully over the frame, as tight as you dare.

Cut another piece of string about a quarter as long again as the longest strut of the kite, and tie it between the two loops on the frame, then tie another loop roughly opposite the intersection of the cross members. This is the kite's bridle (woah there, boy), which is where the string for the flying line is attached. You can make a tail by tying small ribbons or feathers, which children enjoy doing.

BENJAMIN MEE

Freeze ice moulds

✳

THE idea of making ice moulds came to me one frosty November morning as I was emptying ice out of the bird bath. You can make beautiful translucent sculptures with little treasures inside, such as leaves and berries. The simplest ice mould is just a container filled with water, and left outside to freeze. If you want to make something elaborate, you could make a mould out of clay, or sand, and then line it with cling film, and fill the hollow with water. Then you leave it outside to freeze.

MELISSA VIGUIER

Make a rain house

※

IF you have young children you might find yourself wondering how to entertain them, without spending money, when it rains for days on end. One solution I found is to convert my greenhouse into a rain house during the winter months. The great thing about a rain house is that you feel like you're outside, but you're not getting wet.

First of all we had to clear the summer's tomato plants out of the way, so there was space to lay down a big piece of tarpaulin. Then it was just a case of rolling up our sleeves as we made sculptures out of soil, used washable paints to paint on the glass, water pistols to clean them again, then played Pictionary, but using twigs and clay instead of drawing pictures. Before long we were all hungry and so settled down to have a picnic and watch the birds.

MELISSA VIGUIER

Make a scarecrow

※

WE have a new addition to our garden: Eric the scarecrow. He isn't the most appealing of scarecrows. His head is way too big and his legs are too short and fat, but we had fun making him and he livens up our garden. (We don't actually grow anything in it!)

We began by clothes shopping, browsing the charity shops to select the most scarecrow-like outfit, and had conversations such as, 'Do you think a straw hat or a flat cap?' and 'Tweed jacket or tank top?' Then we stopped at the pet shop for a giant pack of straw.

Back home we tied together an old broom handle and a thin branch with string to make a cross frame and draped the clothes on to it, using an old pillowcase for the head and gardening gloves for the hands. Then we stuffed him silly with straw, securing it with string tied at the neck, waist, wrists and ankles. We drew on his face with permanent marker and glued straw on to the inside of his hat so that it poked out like hair. A flower in his buttonhole, and he was ready to be hammered into place.

Of course, you don't have to go for the Worzel Gummidge look. How about a female scarecrow with a nice frock and handbag? A cool dude in bandana and shades? Or a scarecrow on a bench?

CLAIRE POTTER

Make splatter-platter paintings

✳

A lazy Susan is one of those spinning platters that people put in the middle of the dining table to help with passing the sauce, but there is more than one good use for this contraption. Why not use it to make splatter-platter paintings? At least that's what we call them, because you drip runny tempura paint on to a piece of paper Blu-Tacked on to the surface of the spinning lazy Susan and the centrifugal force whirls the paint about.

At this point you may think that this is just a very messy idea, but the results are brilliant, and the process, too. I have two young children, so the best way for everyone to help out was to put the lazy Susan on the floor, cut out a large piece of paper to totally cover the spinning plate, and make a tight fitting cardboard skirt around the lazy Susan (to stop the splatters). My youngest son preferred to be held in a horizontal flying position over the plate, while dropping the paint, but this isn't the only way to get good results.

MELISSA VIGUIER

Gourmet days

Ideas for food-based fun

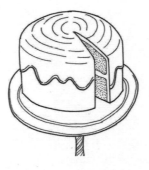

Eat out at home

※

TAKING children to restaurants can sometimes be a trial. To prepare children for a special meal out or just for some fun, set up a restaurant at home. Ask the children to decide on a theme or type of food: Italian or Chinese work quite well. Younger ones can help make decorations for the table, napkins and coloured flags. Older children can write the menu or if you have a small chalkboard do a 'specials list'.

On our Chinese-themed night we bought prawn crackers and sesame toast from the local takeaway and made a child-friendly stir fry (strips of chicken and veg, noodles and soy sauce). The table was laid with chopsticks, paper mats and rice bowls, and to my surprise everyone tucked in. Role-playing different parts can add to the fun, with the children being the waiters and Dad pretending to be the chef!

JOANN LEEDING

Take your own taste test

✳

O UR kids tend to like sweet foods but I didn't realise quite how sweet until we tried a family hot chocolate taste test. Recently we've been flummoxed by all the new brands of hot chocolate (100 per cent Belgian, French, Italian, Spanish, milk, dark, organic ...) on the supermarket shelves and wanted to find one we all liked and could buy without having an international summit first. So we set up a panel of four kids and three adults to test eight of the major brands.

It turned into a proper event with lots of discussion and opinion, and the kids – rather like (I imagine) Stephen Fry doing a spoof wine tasting – were super enthusiastic at detecting multifarious textures (powdery, gritty, cloying) and flavours (rich, milky, fatty, cinnamon, 'mucked around' and sweet – that's super sweet to most adults).

It was great fun debating it, and for perhaps for the first time in their lives, the kids really tuned in to their tastebuds and discovered the subtle flavours in their food. We did it with hot chocolate but you can try it with anything from orange juice to cornflakes. Though personally I'm craving to wean them off the sweet stuff and get their opinion on some savouries such as rice, tomato soup, crisps and baked beans ...

JANE PHILLIMORE

Go to the supermarket

*

IN these days of Ocado and late-night opening, the last thing you ever want to do is drag the children round the supermarket. I don't know what happened the other day, but we got to the point – frozen pitta bread for breakfast – where there was no choice.

I could be grumpy or cheerful, but I managed the latter. The older ones looked at recipes and chose things they would like to eat. They wrote a list each (handwriting practice, hurray!) which included 'beaf, pref. shin' and 'biskits'. When we got there, we kept the baby quiet with a receipt we found on the floor and said was an important list. Her brothers went round like self-important hunter-gatherers. They said out-of-character things such as, 'I think we're out of loo roll', and 'Ah, fish cakes, that would make a nice meal', and I pretended their choices were the ones I'd have made myself (frozen own-brand is probably just as good as fresh organic).

We didn't find 'beaf, pref shin', but when we got home, so transformed were they by the experience, they wanted to cook dinner themselves, and so transformed was I, I let them.

SABINE DURRANT

Eat what you read

※

WHEN my sons were small, large parts of our lives were influenced by our bedtime stories.

'Mummy, what's curds and whey?'

'It's junket, like we have sometimes for pudding, but plain and white instead of fruity and pink.'

'Can we have it tomorrow?'

This was followed over the years by various foods found in our bedtime stories. Bread and milk and blackberries, as eaten by Flopsy, Mopsy and Cottontail, was (and still is) a favourite.

Pemmican (really corned beef) was provided in chunks for expeditions – as in *Swallows and Amazons*.

I was often asked for a posset for tired brains after school; this from *The Box of Delights*: 'A posset,' said the Inspector, 'is a jorum of hot milk, and in that hot milk, Master Kay, you put a hegg, and ... a spoonful of treacle and a grating of nutmeg and you stir 'em well up ... It will make a new man of you, Master Kay, while now you're all worn down with learning.'

HEATHER SHUTE

Make them eat their words

※

FOOD seems to be a great lubricant for learning in our household. It follows that perhaps the most accessible way to get our children to speak another language is to give it to them on a plate, literally. Any language will do, but it does help if there is a defined cuisine associated with the culture.

We chose an Italian meal to introduce Italian words to the children. You would be surprised at how much is already known other than 'pizza' and 'pasta'. Words for utensils are rapidly picked up, together with those for condiments and ingredients.

Verbs associated with speed of consumption can then be applied liberally to dawdlers – 'presto!' – and racers – 'lago!' – if needed. Conversations can even be instigated, together with polite phrases that can be used to win a condescending smile from Italian waiters when eating away from home. Best of all, finding out about language through food guarantees thought-provoking questions ('Did the gladiators eat spaghetti?') and a clean plate at the end of the meal, even with the pickiest of eaters.

VINCENT REID

Make ice cream with salt

✳

By making use of the properties of ice and water and its reaction with salt you can make a little ice cream the old-fashioned way. You will need a small cup with two tablespoons of milk, one of cream and a teaspoon of cocoa powder. Give it a quick stir.

Begin with a large mixing bowl and fill the bottom with roughly crushed ice cubes. Add a couple of tablespoons of salt. Place the cup in the centre of your ice-filled bowl and pack more ice and salt in layers around the cup. Then cover the bowl with a tea towel and leave for about an hour. When you return, the mixture should be frozen – give it a stir and eat.

The water molecules stick very well together to form ice; therefore a lot of heat is required to break those bonds. At 0C, the ice is breaking and forming those bonds all the time as it slowly melts. Adding salt disrupts that process and the energy required by the water to reform as ice is much higher. This energy, or heat, comes from the surrounding air and the cream mixture and is enough to freeze it.

For more kitchen science ideas, visit www.thenakedscientists.com

JOANN LEEDING

Make elderflower cordial

❋

THE elder is a versatile shrub that seems to embody summer and grows in hedgerows, gardens and parks, and on wasteland. The creamy white flowers, which have a unique and unmistakable scent, are said to have medicinal qualities and have been used for centuries to make herbal tea. They can also be made into various drinks, including champagne and cordial, dipped in a light batter and made into tasty fritters, or used to flavour a traditional custard made from eggs and cream. The deep red berries are also versatile and make a wonderful red wine – they are known as the Englishman's grape. But it's the flowers, which can be picked through June and July, that make a delicious elderflower cordial.

Make sure you pick only healthy, fresh blooms – avoid any brown ones or the drink will taste bitter. Infuse 40 flower heads in four pints of boiling water. Add 4lb (1.8kg) of sugar, two sliced lemons and four teaspoons of citric acid, and stir until the sugar has dissolved. Remove any scum that may have risen to the surface and cover with a piece of cotton. Soak for four days, stirring twice daily, and then strain through a fine sieve and decant into sterile bottles. It will store for up to a month in the fridge and can be frozen. For a refreshing drink, dilute in water or for a 5pm treat, mix with vodka and a touch of lemon for a homemade martini.

LYDIA FULTON

51

Make your own ginger beer

※

WHEN my kids have commercially produced carbonated soft drinks, I worry about their teeth. Though my concern is based on sugar levels, there are a host of other ingredients on the label with doubtful-sounding names.

There is one way to ensure you know exactly what goes into your offspring: you can make your own fizzy drink.

In order to make a wonderful ginger beer, free from colouring and additives, you will need a funnel and a clean two-litre plastic bottle with a lid.

First, add one cup of sugar to the bottle. Then, according to taste, finely grate 1½ to 2 tablespoons of root ginger and put this into the bottle. Juice a lemon and pour this into the bottle. Now, add ¼ teaspoon of baking yeast and enough water to three-quarter fill the bottle. Shake the bottle vigorously until the sugar is dissolved and the ingredients are clearly well combined. Now fill the bottle with water but leave a 4cm gap at the top. If you do not do this, the bottle might explode once the yeast does its work. Finally, seal the bottle tightly and put it somewhere warm for 24-48 hours.

You can test the bottle to see if the fermentation process has occurred by squeezing it. If it is rock hard, then you are finished. Place the bottle in the fridge for a few hours, which will stop the yeast from acting. This also stops a ginger beer fountain when you open the bottle. Bubbles can disturb the sediment upon opening, so it is best to use a tea strainer in order to avoid bits of ginger in your drink.

Yeast is a live ingredient that consumes sugars. In the

process it produces carbon dioxide – the bubbles in soft drinks. It is what makes bread rise and creates the alcohol in most alcoholic beverages. There is a trace amount of alcohol in this ginger beer, anywhere from 0.2 per cent to 0.4 per cent in total.

But, best of all, it tastes better than anything you can buy in the supermarket.

VINCENT REID

Make a magic potion

Ingredients for a wet afternoon:
1. Three bored small children
2. Three large utensils (preferably plastic)
3. A handful of spoons
4. The contents of your kitchen cupboard, or fridge.

When I was little, my friend and I used to make magic potions with all the medicine in the bathroom cabinet. Then we used to stir it with her brother's toothbrush. Now I'm grown up I've moved the game to the kitchen.

I take out every bottle from the fridge – milk, ketchup, horseradish, orange juice (preferably past its use-by date), mustard, gherkins and so on, and let the children put a small spoonful or dollop of each into their bowl.

Then we move on to the cupboard and plunder the herbs, curry powder, Nesquik, vinegar, coffee, broken teabags, sugar, Worcestershire sauce, golden syrup, Thai fish paste. Anything.

They smell their mixtures as they go along and splutter and retch and dare each other to taste them. You have to get the correct dry/wet balance. You're after the consistency of runny porridge. Then, when you judge the moment is right – in my house it's when the gagging for more is getting a little too realistic – you produce the final explosive ingredient: bicarbonate of soda. Give them a dessertspoonful each and stand back ...

SABINE DURRANT

Visit a pick-your-own farm

✻

WORRIED about food miles and traceability? Evangelical in your efforts to get your kids to eat a healthy diet? Driven to distraction by their refusal to even acknowledge that vegetables exist? Worry not, for there's a virtually guaranteed solution. When it comes to getting them to eat their greens, kids are suckers for pick-your-own (PYO) although you might have to explain that this involves a visit to a farm and not a nasal cavity.

The beauty of PYO is that you are getting your fruit and veg at the peak of freshness; your kids get to run around and see where food comes from and everyone has a nice time (on a recent visit to a local farm my son discovered that sugar-snap peas are not only a bona fide food item but also taste fabulous raw). Plus it's cheaper than the supermarket.

There are around 600 PYO farms nationwide and an abundance of delicous food to choose from when you get there, though perhaps not all of them can match Parkside Farm in Enfield, Middlesex which was named 2009 Pick Your Own Farm of the Year. It offers 20 different fruit and vegetable crops including six varieties of strawberries, three varieties of raspberry, blackberries, blackcurrants, plums, spinach, onions, cucumbers, tomatoes, courgettes, sweetcorn, squash, French beans, beetroot, and broad beans.

For details of PYO farms near you, call Farma on 0845 4588420 or visit www.farmshopping.net (which also tells you what's in the season).

ABIGAIL FLANAGAN

Hunt for exotic fruits

✳

THERE is a world of fruit at our fingertips that most people have never tasted. Good examples include the divine feijoa, the garish star apple and the bittersweet tamarillo. If you go on a fruit-hunt, you never know what you will find.

Start your morning by giving each child a set budget. I have found that about £8 works well. Then all you do is visit nearby fruit shops and buy all the weird fruit that you have never eaten.

It's best to visit establishments where the names of fruit are displayed so that you can copy their names down. When you get home, you can research your rare delicacies and then vote on which tastes the best.

One drawback is that you might not be able to identify fruit that has gone off until you get it home. You might want to explore why it is that your chosen fruit is not a household name. Could it have something to do with the flavour perhaps?

It's possible that you will uncover something that becomes a favourite treat for life. Whatever the case, fruit hunting is a great morning out with an exciting and healthy snack at the end.

VINCENT REID

Throw a street party

※

IT might sound daunting but, as a group of us have just discovered, organising a street party is easy and a wonderful way to spend a late summer evening. Just select a small group of neighbours to get involved and deliver letters to every house stating your chosen date, a vague itinerary and asking for donations to cover the basics (paying the council for closing the road, bouncy castle, paper plates, cups etc).

Stretch your pool of cash by borrowing necessaries from schools, church halls or play centres in the area. Nearby shops or restaurants might offer to donate food or drink to the cause too (we were surprised how generous they were) and it would be worth finding some free local talent for the occasion.

Everyone can bring drinks and something to throw on a communal barbecue. We had our own self-appointed, cigar-smoking chef who was happy to stand in his front garden decked out with disco lights and cook to order all night. On the big day, clear the cars from a section of the street, bring out your garden furniture and dress the street with bunting for the traditional street-party look. We decided to start at 4pm and let the children run wild on scooters, bikes and bouncy castle (a great investment) while we enjoyed a drink, watching their carefree liberty.

Our street party proved to be a rare and memorable occasion – we have decided to make it an annual fixture in our summer calendar.

FIONA TATHAM

Pick blackberries

✳

IF you want your family to sample the season's wild blackberries, remember to do it before the end of September. Legend has it that Michaelmas, which falls on September 29, is the last date blackberries should be picked because of a curse supposedly placed on the prickly shrub by the devil. September 29 was said to be the day when Lucifer was evicted from heaven by Saint Michael at sword point, and the rebellious angel's fall was broken by a blackberry bush. If you've ever suffered a jag from the bramble, you'll understand why he cursed it. A more prosaic explanation for the deadline is that the berries are past their best by then, and liable to be home to tiny maggots (although climate change seems to be bringing this date forward every year).

Even if you live in a city you should be able to find wild blackberries, which thrive on urban wasteground as well as country lanes, in August and September. Equip the kids with old sandcastle buckets and get them picking; rinse your harvest before you eat it.

HEATHER RICHARDSON

Make apple cobbler

※

As autumn sets in, many English apples will be ready for harvest, making it the perfect time to try out some appley recipes.

If you don't have an orchard or apple tree nearby, then the best source of English apples is farm shops, traditional greengrocers and farmers' markets. For culinary purposes, make sure you pick cooking or dual-purpose apples.

There are many types to choose from – from the traditional Discovery, to the naturally sweeter Annie Elizabeth that is perfect for stewing; or the Blenheim Orange, which has a crumbly texture and can be harvested in late September and stored up until Christmas.

To use up any bruised windfalls, make this simple take on a traditional apple cobbler. Take half a dozen peeled and sliced apples, 1 cup of flour, 1 cup of soft brown sugar, 1 egg, 1 teaspoon of cinnamon and half a cup of melted butter.

Place the apple slices in the bottom of a greased 20cm baking tray. In a separate bowl stir the flour, sugar and cinnamon together, then mix in the whisked egg and sprinkle this topping over the apples. Cover it with the melted butter and bake in a hot oven for 30 minutes. Served warm with clotted cream this makes the perfect autumn treat.

LYDIA FULTON

Make slow coffee

✳

ANY time you step inside a cafe with the kids, you can wave goodbye to a tenner. So, inspired by economy and the example of my Dutch friend Nienke, who's elevated elevenses into an art form, I've decided to make 'slow coffee' at home instead. All you need is espresso coffee, hot chocolate powder, a medium pan, a fork or whisk, and milk. While the coffee is brewing, heat the milk, whisking gently and patiently until it's a storm of bubbles (about five minutes). Then pour the coffee into cups, scoop over the milky froth and sprinkle a little chocolate powder on top. The kids' favourites are usually super-bubbly hot chocolate or occasionally a 'babycino' of hot frothy milk. They love sprinkling on tiny marshmallows, grated chocolate or hundreds and thousands using cardboard cut-outs in the shapes of their initials, faces or numbers. Just add some home-made muffins (go to www.heartandhome.net and search for 'basic muffins') and relax.

JANE PHILLIMORE

Bake a cake

※

'No, you can't have another biscuit, but you can help me make cakes.' The children eagerly wash their hands, for once. It's not just the end result that appeals to them but the chance to get their hands on all those mysterious packets out of their reach in the kitchen cupboards.

We leaf through cookery books until they spot the iced fairy cakes; so we get the tins and they fill two trays with paper cases. I give them a bowl each to avoid arguments and then hand out wooden spoons which they use to have an impromptu sword fight while I measure out the butter and sugar.

A lot of the flour ends up on them, turning them into small apparitions, and with the introduction of the eggs, the excitement increases. Theo cracks the first, breaking it successfully but not quite managing to get the contents into the bowl. Ava's technique is more visceral, crushing the egg in her palm and watching it stream through her fingers. She prods the yolk until it breaks and licks her finger. I guess we won't be offering these to guests ...

I whisk the cakes into the oven while the children settle down to their favourite pastime: scraping the bowls.

My grandmother used to let me do this whenever she was baking and would joke afterwards: 'I don't need to wash that bowl.' Now, I watch my own two, in complete silence, repeating the ritual.

AMANDA WOODARD

Let the kids cook dinner

*

THE 12-year-old knows some Brownies, who did a badge to cook an omelette, and like to play restaurants. So: 'Mum, can Lillie and Becks and I cook dinner for all our parents?' Fab development. I foresee many happy years of being waited on hand and foot. I was to be coordinateuse and consultant, and my main duty (after lugging them round the shops and paying) was to stay out of it.

There was a recipe book, and a timeline written out (by them) like Christmas at Delia's. The menu took some weeks of discussion and evolved into something rather sophisticatedly Mexican, with tortillas done in the oven, grated cheese, home-made guacamole and salsa, chilli con carne, rice and sour cream. They chose Mexican beer to match, and elegant candles. I only occasionally shrieked at them to clean as they went.

The adults were in no-cooking hog heaven: we made friends out of acquaintances, and stayed up till two. The youth were hugely amused and rather pleased with themselves, and they all stayed the night. The meal was delicious. The kitchen looked like we'd had the drunk, hyperactive, food-fetish psycho-vandals in to decorate.

LOUISA YOUNG

Eat sweet chestnuts

※

SWEET chestnuts have prickly cases, like a hedgehog, that crack open when the nuts inside are ripe. December is the best month to forage for them as they fall to the ground when it is cold. They can then be eaten raw or cooked.

To make roasted sweet chestnuts, cut a slit into each nut then pop them under a grill, into an oven or wrap them in foil to sit among the cinders of an open fire for about 20 minutes. They are a tasty, warm winter snack and great with your Christmas dinner.

Or to make sweet chestnut puree, cut a slit into 1kg of chestnuts and place them in a pan of boiling water for 10 minutes, then remove from the water and peel the chestnuts whilst they are still warm. Put them into a pan with a pint of milk and cook for 45 minutes. Drain the chestnuts and push them through a sieve until they are smooth, then mix into 100g of butter and enjoy! The puree is delicious spread on toast for cosy, winter breakfasts.

LYDIA FULTON

Dress for high tea

❋

BOOKS of etiquette were a must in Edwardian society. They were as essential for day-to-day living as spats on a muddy street. Thankfully, those days are long gone, but much joy can be had in recreating the past on your own terms.

The first rule of high tea is that one must look the part. Half the fun is dressing up. Get everyone into their most over-the-top Ascot gear, complete with absurd hats for the girls and pocket watches made of paper for the boys.

The tea itself should be one of the old-fashioned sorts with a name that reeks of the colonial days, such as Earl Grey, Assam or Ceylon. Remember that the milk always goes in first to avoid cracking the bone china. Needless to say, modern fruit teas are unacceptable.

Of course, no high tea is complete without a selection of jams, scones and ginger snaps. It would take a dedicated fan of the genre to make all these items in the kitchen for the express purpose of high tea. Thankfully, supermarkets can be coopted into providing the edibles. But it would ruin the overall effect to leave them in their packets.

The icing on the cake is to speak as if one were talking to royalty. You may think that this will be too difficult for younger children, but I have found that they learn quickly if jam scones with cream on top are the reward.

VINCENT REID

Have a French breakfast

✳

WHEN my father was young, my grandmother used to preside over a weekly French-only tea, so now we're trying out *le petit dejeuner français* with our six-year-old, who recently started learning French at school, and her little brother. Our local bakery sells good croissants so we can bring some animal-training techniques to bear on our children's development. If a sealion will clap its flippers for fish, we reason, our kids will talk French for croissants. Conversation is lively, if limited. We can ask each other how we are (*Comme ci, comme ça* seems to be the favourite diagnosis, followed by *Ca va mal*), and count the croissants, and discuss colours.

Even this is magical. There's no better way to appreciate diversity than to call 'milk' and 'bread' by another name, with a different set of meanings and a different culture surrounding it. It's like peeking through a crack into a new world. Eventually the crack will become a door.

Not that this world is altogether new. A two-year-old inevitably finds it easier to say *je veux croissant* than *un croissant, s'il vous plait*, and there have already been disputes over pronunciation and grammar. *Comment tu t'appelles?* Or Comment t'appells tu? Could I have been saying it wrong all these years? *Enfin*, time for *un verre*.

JAMES RUSSELL

Green-fingered days

Activities for young gardeners

Sow your own seeds

❋

IN spring, we set about sowing the seeds that will turn our garden into a summer haven for cherry tomatoes, towering sunflowers, trailing edible nasturtiums and runner beans. They're all easy to grow, and it's an activity my kids love to do with friends around the kitchen table.

All you need is a few packets of seeds, a bag of seed or potting compost, a seed tray with a lid and a water spray.

We recycle plastic vegetable trays (mushroom ones are good). Make drainage holes if they don't already have them. Half-fill the seed tray with compost, allowing time for compost-fondling. Then place your seeds in a row with 2.5cm gaps between each row. Cover the seeds with around 1.5cm of compost. We write our names and what we've planted on masking tape and stick it to the tray.

Get the kids to mist the compost thoroughly with the water spray, pop the lid on and place the trays in front of a window. My children keep theirs in their bedrooms so it's easy to remember to water them when they get up and go to bed. Germination times vary but usually something appears between one and two weeks. The shriek of excitement at the sight of the first seedling is matched only by the whining envy of the siblings whose seeds have yet to germinate.

SHARON SWEENEY-LYNCH

Identify weeds and flowers

✳

THERE is no clear reason why a flower is classed as a weed or vice versa. Yet even small children make the distinction. Finding out what kids name a weed or a flower – and why – makes for a great morning in the garden. In our house, it was clear that anything growing in the lawn was a weed as was anything with stings or thorns (except roses). Challenging these preconceptions is where the fun begins. Why not add dandelion hearts and leaves to your green salad? You can make stinging nettle soup, provided that everyone wears gloves when harvesting. Soon a weed will be anything in the lawn that you can't eat.

VINCENT REID

Start a sunflower race

※

SUNFLOWERS are one of the easiest plants to grow. You just throw the seeds into a pot of soil and make sure you water them every couple of days. Sunflowers grow at a rapid rate. This means that the kids can track their growth on a daily basis and compete in a sunflower race that compares the results on designated 'measure days'. The grower with the tallest plant wins a prize.

Strategy can come into play if every race entrant has three or four plants. You can allow the kids to place their seedlings in different locations around the house to see which one grows the fastest. Of course, everyone needs a prize, so awards can be made for 'most growth', 'most unique' and 'most deformed'. The end of the growing year comes rapidly. In the space of a few months, you will have transformed your children into green-fingered gurus.

VINCENT REID

Take time-delay photographs

※

F ED up with the kids' constant nagging to have everything right here, right now, I wanted to try something that would require patience and a bit of delayed gratification. They were sceptical, but brightened up when I offered temporary custody of the digital camera. The idea is simple – take a picture of the garden or a favourite beauty spot at regular intervals, from exactly the same vantage point. You could do this every day for a month or once a month for a year. When you compare the photos the differences will be striking. My 10-year-old twins captured a series of close-up shots of an emerging bulb over a few weeks. They were amazed at the daily changes, which saw it morph from a green shoot to a colourful flower, which bloomed spectacularly then faded. We uploaded the photos on to the computer and printed them out on cheap paper. Laying them out in sequence, we could appreciate how nature was changing right in front of our eyes, but at a rate so slow we wouldn't normally have perceived it.

LESLEY CARR

Become an urban botanist

※

THERE'S a game we've been playing for years. We call it 'count the cans'. It's played outdoors on a piece of wasteland at the end of our street, where, for a long time, we've been promised a park. But ever since we've lived here, it's been wasteland for litter.

My kids count the different cans: Coke (two), Fanta (three), Lilt (one), beer (eight). Beer always wins. The next round is plastic bags: Tesco (seven), bags from the local store (four), and so on.

But now we've a new game – finding wild flowers. Since being given a copy of the beautifully illustrated *A Little Guide to Wild Flowers*, we've become urban botanists. This children's guide doesn't just identify flora that flourishes in hedgerows lining country lanes, but in the middle of big cities too. There are pictures of weeds and plants that grow out of half-derelict walls and push up between the cracks in the pavements.

Guide in hand, within minutes we'd spotted sowthistle, ragwort and spurge on our wasteland. We'd learned the difference between stinging nettles and white dead-nettle, crucial as one stings and the other doesn't. We didn't know we lived among so much nature. Now we've mastered urban botany, we're moving on to birds.

DEA BIRKETT

A Little Guide to Wild Flowers by Charlotte Voake is published by Eden Project Books.

73

Garden at the grandparents' house

✳

GRANDCHILDREN are beloved but exhausting and finding ways to amuse them while visiting frail grandparents can be challenging for everyone. But this can all improve with the climate.

Gardening at the grandparents' house would score big with Supernanny. It's a socially useful pursuit helping the elderly who find the task increasingly burdensome, and it's healthy and educational. And, if, as is so often the case, it furnishes your kids with unexpected pocket money, then it's a great way of both instilling a work ethic and lining their pockets.

One recent day spent with the grandparents transformed their small, suburban back garden. The kids fed and planted grass in those patchy, shady corners, forlorn from lack of light. A mouse (my son, prone to exaggeration, swears it was a rat) and a toad were unearthed in the small dumping ground by the bins, long overdue a clear out.

The children learned to identify lavender and basil, and the nine-year-old lost his mowing virginity to a 446 Hovertrim.

We had insisted the kids would garden for free, so grandma slipped them a few quid with their glasses of lemonade when we weren't looking. Grandad, loitering to wave us off, passed a fiver through the back window with a nod and a wink, thinking he was so clever. I can still remember the euphoria induced when, unbeknown to my parents and each other, Grandma and Grandad would both slip us pocket money. Double quids in all round!

JOANNE MALLABAR

Grow your own farm

※

IMAGINE a farm so small that it can grow on your windowsill. We begin with a seed tray and a couple of centimetres of compost in the bottom. Next we use some pebbles to make the stone walls around the fields – this divides the tray into four fields. Then we have a rummage for seeds. We have had great success with bird seed, and seeds intended for sprouting, such as alfalfa. Then we scatter the seeds quite densely in the four fields, cover them with a thin layer of compost and water them. We don't have a mini-watering can, so made holes in the lid of a jam jar. Then the tray is placed on a sunny windowsill, and the toy animals are set free on their farm, and the whole thing is watered every day.

The beauty of a mini-farm is it's low maintenance; you can plant the crops at any time of year, and when the plants grow bigger than the toy animals you call in a mini-combine harvester (or a pair of scissors).

MELISSA VIGUIER

Plant garlic

✳

PLANTING garlic is so simple and quick that it's a great way to introduce kids to growing plants and vegetables.

All you need is a few bulbs of garlic. Carefully separate each one into cloves – anything smaller than 1cm in diameter should be discarded. Then push them, pointed end up, just below the surface of the soil in a sunny part of the garden. Keep the cloves 10cm-18cm apart – the bigger the gap, the better the yield. If you don't have a garden, use ordinary potting compost and one clove per small pot and place on a sunny window sill, balcony or patio.

All you need to do then is water the cloves if the weather is very dry and, in the spring, feed them once or twice a month with general-purpose fertiliser. By the summer you will be in business. You can plant garlic anytime between late autumn and early spring.

HELEN DAVIES

Visit a botanic garden

＊

BOTANIC gardens might not sound like a great place to take small children but they are. Our two, Alasdair, five, and Katie, two, love to visit the gardens in Cambridge, which boast some magnificent pine trees, a lake with ducks and stepping stones, and a knee-high grass maze to run around. The children can pretty much have the run of the grass areas and the garden is free of dogs. Within minutes of arrival we were at the lake and ready to feed the ducks who were soon joined by moorhens and coots.

Opened in 1846, the gardens are in the heart of Cambridge, close to the rail station and university science departments. The last time we visited we took a picnic and enjoyed a tour round the glasshouses when the weather turned wet. Inside, we found a banana tree, coffee plant and our daughter's favourite: a fishpond. She stayed quiet for 10 whole minutes watching the fish. Perfect!

To find a botanic gardens near to you, go to the website of Botanic Gardens Conservation International (www.bgci.org/garden_search.php) where you'll find a list of 116 gardens across the UK.

JOANN LEEDING

Grow a garden in the kitchen

✳

ONE day we discovered a green shoot pushing out of a piece of root ginger left behind the fruit bowl. The kids were amazed. This strange development meant that the ugly lumpy thing was actually alive! We decided to find out what would happen if we gave it a bit more encouragement. After checking out best practice on the internet, we laid the ginger on top of some damp compost and left it in a shady spot. Soon leaves had emerged, and two months on it was 66cm tall.

We wondered how many other things could be found in the kitchen that could be grown into something. A quick survey of the shelves yielded some likely contenders: poppy, fennel, sunflower and pumpkin seeds. The children set up a row of little pots and laid bets on which would germinate first. You can also sit carrot tops and the leafy top bit of a pineapple in dishes of water, where they'll continue to sprout for weeks. My friend has a plant grown from a grapefruit seed planted 20 years ago.

Apart from being fun, growing a garden from things in the kitchen introduces children to success and failure (not everything will work – let them find out for themselves) and it helps them understand that the things we eat were originally grown by somebody else, somewhere else.

LESLEY CARR

Create an indoor garden

✳

IF the thought of cultivating a plot in the garden sounds like hard labour to your children, then creating a miniature garden might have far more appeal, particularly for young children – and you can always bring it indoors on chilly or rainy days.

First, find a rigid, shallow container of any size or shape and fill nearly to the brim with any old soil or sand. This is the foundation on which to build your garden. For example, to make an orchard of convincing winter trees, get a bunch of grapes and eat them. Take the denuded stalk, upend it, and stick it into the earth. An old, small mirror from a vanity case makes a convincing pond; disguise the sharp edges of your pond with little bits of moss found growing in the cracks in walls and paving stones – the moss also makes a better-looking lawn than you'll ever see in your own back garden.

In the past, we have used herbs, such as parsley, to make a rather fetching border hedge and made a garden path by collecting tiny pebbles or shells and laying them like a mosaic on the earth. The stamens from flowers can make an excellent miniature flowerbed and you can add a swing, a greenhouse or a gazebo using twigs, lolly sticks or cut-up plastic water bottles: the possibilities are endless. Scour the park or garden with your children for inspiration and let your imagination run wild.

AMANDA WOODARD

Daring days

Sleuthing, sleepovers, secrets and survival!

Make an ancient treasure map

✳

A NY decent treasure map worth its barrel of sea salt needs to look like it's been washed out to sea in a bottle and recovered from the worldly possessions of a recently deceased vagabond. There's no point taking a permanent marker to a blank sheet of A4 and telling your children that the still wet sketching holds the secrets to golden riches – even a three-year-old will see through that.

Luckily, a tea bag, some cooking oil and a little time is all you need to make your treasure map look as though it was once in the clutches of Long John Silver himself.

Take a piece of white paper and sketch your map – don't forget that X marks the spot. For authenticity you should add compass points and maybe some kind of riddle or clues hinting at the treasure's location. Tear away at the edges randomly for a ragged effect. Now liberally wipe the wet tea bag across both sides of the paper to give it ye olde brown tint. Squish the map into a ball and let it dry overnight.

In the morning, carefully open the map, and wipe both sides with a little cooking oil, wiping off excess. Give it an hour – just enough time for you to put on your prosthetic hook and perfect your 'Aar, me hearties' – and you should have a faded brown, ancient-looking document that should fool any toddler.

ANTONY JONES

Make your own treasure hunt

✳

CHILDREN always love a good treasure hunt. However, my children are a bit young for the traditional written clues so we have invented our own non-literary treasure hunt that encourages observation skills instead.

Tour the house and garden with a digital camera and take photos of familiar and not so familiar objects such as toys, pieces of furniture, flowers, books and pictures. Moving targets can be a real challenge to find, so photograph the pets if you have any. Make sure the treasure hunt isn't too easy by taking pictures of displaced items such as shoes in toy boxes.

Experiment with your photography and take obscure images, close-ups that need careful scrutiny to identify and abstract shots.

After you have taken enough photos – obviously the length of the treasure hunt depends on the amount of photos taken – print out the images. Set up your hunt (while the children are engaged elsewhere) as you would a traditional treasure hunt and carefully hide the photos around the house leaving each new photo/clue with the previous object. Make sure the hunt involves as much exercise as possible by leaving photos downstairs that involve running upstairs, etc. The treasure, as always, should be left with the last object. I find that our cat is the best photo to end with as he really could be anywhere and can keep the children eagerly looking for a long time. Do make sure the treasure is not too disappointing – I have made that mistake – something edible and sweet always seems to work.

FIONA TATHAM

Check your emergency kit

✳

WHAT'S in your emergency kit? The bare necessities of life are available in most houses. We are all accustomed to having heat, water and electricity on demand. Without these things, we would be quite helpless. But what if something went wrong, such as a power cut or a broken pipe? It is worth discussing with the children what you need and why. It may come as a shock that we are dependent on these amenities. After discarding the suggestions of favourite DVDs, our emergency kit ended up as a box of matches, candles, a blanket, two tins of beans, a pocket knife (with tin opener attachment), some spoons and a big chocolate bar. A few days later, we had to use it for the first time when the power went off. It was a remarkable success.

VINCENT REID

Send semaphore signals

※

KIDS love codes and secret messages. One way to send codes between two people is to use semaphore signalling. Each person needs two sticks with A4 pieces of paper stuck to them in order to make flags. You can make your own alphabet or find the accepted signals on Wikipedia (en.wikipedia. org/wiki/semaphore_flags). Armed with a copy of your flag positions, you can both go to a park or nearby field. The first few messages will take a while to understand but the mistakes are part of the fun. After a short period of time you will find that complex messages can be sent relatively quickly. Added benefits are that it provides a good aerobic workout and it lets you wave a flag without nationalist connotations.

VINCENT REID

Pitch a tent indoors

✳

IMAGINE camping without biting insects, toilet dramas, rocks or leaky tents – with the best bits left in. Well, this it what our family call 'indoor camping'. Starting off with a strong length of rope, we tied one end around the wardrobe and the other around the chest of drawers, then slung sheets and fabric over the top to make two triangle tents. We threw in duvets, cushions and a torch. As the sun set we gathered the last of our essentials, which included a bucket of water, a saucepan, matches and the stove, plates, cutlery and food.

Dinner consisted of pasta and salad and then we had a good natter. The bucket of water was used for washing up. It was messy but we tidied up and wriggled into our tents.

When morning came, and sunlight shone in, the illusion of being on a camping adventure no longer seemed plausible, but don't those fleeting experiences often seem the most magical?

MELISSA VIGUIER

Swap houses for the weekend

※

IT'S great to go and stay with friends or family who have children, but it can also be great – and an altogether different kind of fun – to stay in someone else's house when they're not there.

We swapped houses with friends in Bristol one weekend, and with my sister in Norwich another – nice city breaks for us who live in a small rural town, and because we did it with friends and family, there wasn't the stress of living in a stranger's house. The accommodation was free, we didn't have to make an effort to be good guests, and we were free to explore the area at our own pace.

Our children loved living in the shoes of other children – playing with their toys, watching their videos, feeding their fish, having a bath with their bath toys, choosing a book to read at bedtime from their bookshelf, sleeping in their beds and eating their cereal in the morning (they were delighted to find Coco Pops). Just being in a different kind of house was interesting to them – an awful lot of time was spent going up and down the ladder to the loft conversion in the Norwich house.

To add to the whole holiday feeling, we all got our children to prepare a 'welcome pack' for the children coming to stay, with information and drawings of good places to go locally and anything else they thought would be helpful. My sister and I even arranged to 'swap' babysitters so that we could each have a night out on the town.

CLAIRE POTTER

Write your own Da Vinci code

✳

HAVE you looked for the code in Leonardo da Vinci's paintings and only seen visions of delivery men with cash-loaded wheelbarrows making repeated trips to Dan Brown's house? You're not alone – but there is a bona fide Da Vinci code that you and the kids can decipher. The all-round genius habitually wrote personal notes in right-to-left 'mirror writing', possibly to hide his thoughts from the Catholic church or, more likely, because he was left-handed and the ink would have easily smudged if he wrote normally.

Apparently, only one in 6,500 people can write backwards naturally due to an 'atypical language centre' in the brain ... but there are ways to master it. One option is to hold a pen in each hand, writing with your preferred side, while imitating the movement with the other – but that's probably best suited to ambidextrous sorts (and who wouldn't give their right arm to be ambidextrous?). Another is to hold paper to your chest or forehead while standing in front of a mirror – now write in a way that is legible as you see it. Easiest of all, however, is to write normally on near-transparent paper, flip it over, and trace the text – voila!

ANTONY JONES

Make a secret code

✳

WRITING in code was a popular pastime among my friends when we were growing up. There were several versions, but the one I designed, and liked the best, was a secret picture language.

You begin by making a list of all the things (nouns) that you regularly describe in secret communications. For instance, these could be the secret places you meet and the code names for everyone in your group – and, of course, the names of the villains. Then make a symbol picture for each one of these people and things. It must be something simple that you will be able to draw easily. Then make a list of verbs: running, meeting, arriving, leaving, chasing, escaping, avoiding and so on, and make a symbol picture for each of these. And don't forget the describing words (adjectives), such as haunted, dangerous, dusty, squashed.

Then move on to numbers. The ancient Egyptians made numbers very simple by making a symbol for just 1, 10, 100, 1,000, 10,000 and 100,000. Then to make the number three, they would simply draw three lots of the symbol for 1. Then string the pictures together on the page to make picture sentences. And if you suspect your code has been deciphered by a villain, change it immediately.

MELISSA VIGUIER

Organise a sleepover

✳

IF you're planning a sleepover, the following hard-earned tips should aid a restful night:

Keep numbers low. You'll soon discover the frenetic factor rapidly increases with each additional guest. Let the children help get the sleeping area ready, with mattresses, airbeds, sofa cushions and whatever else comes to hand. Make sure everyone's got enough room, and any makeshift tent arrangements aren't going to collapse in the middle of the night.

Fix the rules of engagement early on and involve the kids in deciding the limits. Tell them what time you'll expect them to quieten down, and give them a clock so they know where they are in the plan.

Excitement levels will be high, but some clever forethought will channel the energy into something non-destructive. Try a treasure hunt, a game of charades, craft activities or a film.

Midnight feasts have universal appeal, though in our house they happen way before the stroke of 12pm. The children assemble their own food and scoff away, tucked up in their sleeping bags. Just for once, forget about the crumbs, and remember no one's teeth fell out because they missed one brushing. Sweet dreams!

LESLEY CARR

Do a world tour in the UK

✳

WHEN we told the lollipop lady we were going to climb Everest in the summer holidays she let the traffic pile up to check she had heard right. Only the day before, the children had been boasting about their planned fishing trip to New Zealand, and on Tuesday they had told her no one should fly because it speeds up climate change.

One year on, we've managed to visit more than 40 countries without taking a single flight, travelling around Britain looking for experiences that remind us of somewhere else. This sort of grand tour relies more on imagination than brochures. In London, there are noodles to be eaten in Chinatown, the Bangladeshi mela to be enjoyed in Brick Lane, boating at Little Venice, and Thai rickshaws in Covent Garden.

Trying to find the world out of town was even better. We made it to Nepal by climbing Skiddaw in the Lake District. And we ate refried beans camping Chilean-style by Ullswater.

Best of all, we've got a lot left to see – there are 194 countries (195 including the Vatican), so at 40 stop-offs a year, this plane-free adventure should keep my family busy for another five years.

NICOLA BAIRD

Get mapping

※

IF you've got a long car drive ahead, then try a bit of role reversal to keep the kids amused. Children love to feel grown-up, so we have passed the task of navigating on holiday to our six-year-old son ... Mad? Well, not quite.

First stop, the internet and www.multimap.com; we plugged in our home postcode and the postcode of our destination in Dorset. A detailed list of instructions appeared and we printed off the document. The instructions list every turn and junction so you may find it helpful to pare them down a bit. We also spent some time adding in service station stops or places of interest from a general road map. The children amused themselves looking out for blue and brown road signs to tick off the list as we travelled along. There is also a useful English lesson here too: 'Mummy, what does 'bear left' mean? I don't think they mean a real bear?!'

Multimap will pick the shortest route between two points, therefore if you are looking for a scenic drive you may need to devise your own route map. It is worth the effort, though, to stop the fighting ... and it almost works!

JOANN LEEDING

Get lost in an 'amaizing' maze

✳

A field may not sound the most promising venue for a day of family fun, but when it's a field of corn as high as an elephant's eye, with a cunning plan cut into it, believe me, it is.

Our destination: Dymchurch in Kent, on a grey day we hoped would clear up but didn't. Our challenge: an ingenious maize maze. Armed with a flag on a pole (sensibly supplied so staff can find and rescue visitors if need be), we set out into the corn along tracks that were not so much paths as mud slides. As the rain bucketed down, staying upright became a bigger challenge than finding our way. It didn't matter. We were happy just being out in the countryside, lost to the world, slip-sliding this way and that, getting covered in mud. If we made it out by teatime, well, that was fine.

There are only a couple of months (generally July to early September) between the corn being high enough to hide in and harvest time, but happily that coincides with the school holidays and there are maize mazes the length and breadth of Britain, from Cornwall to Stirling, Pembrokeshire to Norfolk. To find one near you, go to www.maizemaze.com. It's the most fun you can have getting lost.

ANDREA CHAPMAN

Hop on a bus

✳

MOST parents believe that taking small children on bus journeys is nothing short of an endurance test. This is, of course, a state of mind. Living in London, where driving is frankly terrifying and tubes involve far too many stairs and escalators, I had no option but to turn to the buses. After a while, I started to see our journeys as a positive and joyful way of spending time and a great way to explore the city.

Just sitting on a bus is exciting and can, depending on the route, serve as a lesson in social anthropology or act as a venue for making friends. Make sure you're prepared for any eventuality: sweets for bribery, drinks, sandwiches. Short rides can show you a city's attractions – we used to take the No 3 bus to Oxford Circus, via Big Ben, Trafalgar Square and Regent Street. Trips that take in a park, residential areas, a few shops, local landmarks, perhaps a fire station or police station are just as rewarding.

Be careful to keep the ride short, however, as you don't want to exhaust the children's enthusiasm before the return journey.

You can find bus maps for most UK cities on the internet (www.tfl.gov.uk has routes for any bus in London) or you could just jump on the first bus and see where it takes you.

FIONA TATHAM

Play at being a super spy

＊

L ILY's mission impossible: covert surveillance of her home with a view to solving the identity of evil Dr Horrible.

10am: Mr X is at the door. Sweat spatters his brow as if he's been running from someone ... or something. Mini detective 005 checks her watch and makes a note that Dad is back from his run.

10.15am: At control centre (the computer), 005 calls up aerial images of The Crescent, her street. Committing them to memory she severs the link – Dr Horrible may be monitoring Google Earth and could track her down.

10.25am: 005 discovers a letter on the doormat. It is addressed to M.

10.28am: Armed with binoculars, 005 slips out the front door in time to see a uniformed individual (the postman?) disappear round the corner. The street is now empty.

11am: Convinced she has unearthed a conspiracy involving Mr X, the postman and the mysterious Dr Horrible, 005 calls M from the mobile for a debriefing. She lets it ring twice, disconnects and rings again. This is the agreed signal for a Code Red. M answers on the second ring of the second call. 005 is tired and hungry. At the debrief, clasping a peanut butter toastie, a terrifying thought crosses 005's mind: could M be Dr Horrible?

JOANNE MALLABAR

Go scavenging

✳

I N those fuzzy hours between 6 and 8am, before most people are awake, Lily (aged three) and I go treasure hunting. We live in a large block of Victorian flats. Nearby are cramped parks; the kind of patchy lawn that has been squeezed in to fulfil a quota of inner-city community space rather than anything more aspirational. It is surprisingly easy to avoid the condoms, syringes and broken beer bottles.

Armed with a magnifying glass, a carrier bag and a tangible sense of anticipation, Lily combs the lawns for treasures. Our booty is always better if the previous day's weather has been clement. To anyone else, the trifles we uncover may seem worthless. To Lily, each is an odyssey of the new. Last week, in one haul, we found a cyclist's drinks cannister, a rainbow Scoobidou, a silver earring and 50p.

On another day, there were fewer man-made artefacts. Instead we found two dead ladybirds. They appeared to have shed their mortal coil either mating or sparring – under the close inspection of the magnifying glass their legs were entwined and fixed with rigor mortis. If we find objects we suspect someone might return for, we place them prominently on top of a railing or on a park bench. Otherwise, the stash is Lily's – all Lily's.

JOANNE MALLABAR

Have a power cut

※

I have vivid childhood memories of the sense of adventure that surviving without electricity during a power cut gave us. So I decided to try it out on my family. I reasoned that this would also enable us to think more about our electricity consumption, and how life was before electricity. But I have to admit the thought of reading our SAS handbook by candlelight, and really having to use our wits to survive had a very real appeal, too!

We had a couple of days to prepare our supplies, to purchase some gas for the camping stove, and stock up on candles, paraffin and matches, and build up morale among the less committed family members.

Then the challenge began! It took nearly an hour to heat a pan of water per person for washing in the morning; then we made porridge, which we ate in the garden because it was too dark indoors. After washing up with cold water, we decided to cook our lunch outside. Lunch had to be dug up first; unfortunately, this wasn't the best of harvests, so we had potato and onion soup, which took half an hour to prepare, and two hours to cook. Before we knew it, it was time to go for a walk and find some food for dinner without visiting any shops because they would be using electricity. We were unsuccessful, not being up to speed on our bush-tucker heritage, so decided to resort to another potato and onion soup. By 4pm it was dark, we hadn't prepared the paraffin lamp, and so had to work by candlelight – eventually the soup and lamp were prepared, time for a spot of storytelling and sleep.

MELISSA VIGUEIR

Go trainspotting

※

Most young children like playing with trains, but my two-year-old enjoys watching them too. We live a few minutes' walk from a suburban station, and when he's grumpy we go down there and sit on the platform.

Admittedly, it isn't much of a station. Once there was a splendid footbridge but that is long gone. A metal shelter offers passengers protection from the elements, but we sit bundled up on an exposed bench and wait. Nothing happens. We chat about the trains we are going to see, count crows and look for planes. My son is patience personified. Half an hour passes and he is still perfectly happy. Suddenly a signal turns from red to green. The rails start to hum. We hold our breath. Will the train have trucks or coaches?

Will it be a huge one or a tiny one? The local bus-on-rails trundles into view and stops. We say hello to the people getting off and then wave as the train departs. A minute later a woman comes breathlessly up the ramp. 'I thought I'd missed it,' she says. 'Then I saw you.'

'I'm afraid you have missed it,' I tell her, embarrassed. 'We're not waiting for a train.'

She looks confused.

'We watching trains,' my son says importantly. He peers down the track, looking out for the next one.

JAMES RUSSELL

Go metal detecting

✳

Many children announce that they are 'off looking for treasure', but little do they realise that they could actually make a buck if they do. The Portable Antiquities Scheme means that if you discover gold or silver more than 300 years old, then it is yours and you can sell it to the country (visit www.finds.org.uk for further details and laws covering Scotland).

All you need is a metal detector, but you can uncover archaeology when weeding the garden or walking in the countryside. If you are serious about finding treasure, it's a good idea to find an affable farmer. Many farmers are quite happy for you to go metal detecting on their fields, so long as you split any profits 50-50 with them.

Societies and amateur archaeology clubs abound throughout the UK (see www.fid.newbury.net for clubs in your area), and metal detectors are available in a range of sizes.

The greatest joy of metal detecting with children is that 'treasure' is anything with an easily identifiable history. Who held this all that time ago and what were they like? How did it get to be here? Was it lost or was it hidden on purpose? This moment of discovery, which creates a connection between the present and the past, is the real treasure.

VINCENT REID

Cultural days

Introducing the arts

Listen to classical music

✳

I wanted to share with my granddaughter the music I love (the stuff we have to call classical because there is no other name) and, after dithering, fell back on the obvious: Prokofiev's *Peter and the Wolf*. Good story, good musical characterisation: oboe as the duck, clarinet as the cat, bassoon as the grandfather (I don't feel a bit like a bassoon myself, but let that pass), three horns as the wolf. We escaped from her younger sister to the room at the top of the house, the one with the decent hi-fi. There I sat, with Ailis, five, snuggled by me. This could be a day of revelation for my first grandchild, my fond gift to the next generation. Next stop, I thought, Monteverdi and John Adams.

My joy was total; hers less so. I blame the wolf. Those three horns worried her. As the wolf prepared to pounce on the innocent duck, she climbed up my arm and buried her face in my neck. I thought I'd loved her fear away but that night she had terrible wolf dreams. We are now about to start therapy with 50-year-old stories about Clever Polly and the Stupid Wolf. The next music session at the top of the house will feature late Beethoven quartets. No pictures. No wolves.

DAVID WARD

Discover a new catchphrase

✳

A month before my mum died, when she had Alzheimer's disease, we were walking along the seafront at Hunstanton with my daughter, Nell, who was demanding to be carried. My mother, hazy about events of a few days ago, her childhood still vivid, remembered a catchphrase her father often used to say: 'I can't pick you up, I've got a bone in my leg.' I've since used this with some success on my five-year-old ('But, Daddy, everyone has a bone in their leg!').

It's essential for dads to have a stock of catchphrases and the kids don't recognise them if you nick them from old TV shows. I've taken to adapting CJ's line from *The Rise and Fall of Reginald Perrin*, telling the kids: 'I didn't get where I am today by refusing to wear trousers!' or 'I didn't get where I am today by wearing pants on my head.'

We often watched *Maggie and the Ferocious Beast* together and I regularly use the Beast's 'Great Googly Moogly!' And we still refer to all younger children as 'dumb babies!' after Angelica in *Rugrats*. When putting the children to bed I've taken to using the catchphrase, 'They tuck you, up your mum and dad' from the poet Adrian Mitchell.

Charles Dickens was right – when we're dead what our kids will remember will be those idiosyncratic sayings we used to bore them with. In fact, I didn't get where I am today without knowing the value of a family catchphrase.

PETE MAY

Visit a library

※

OUR teenage girls' reaction to the suggestion of a trip to the library is not printable. Young people are reading less, yet libraries have changed for the better. In the age of the shopping mall, we had forgotten the joy of delving into books for nothing.

The internet section of our library was eye-catching: stylishly decorated, and filled with the latest computers and coffee aroma. This visit was about books, though, and we challenged the girls to find a tome that would inspire another family member. The informality was refreshing – signs marked 'silence' are long gone – and there's a busy events calendar.

Libraries hold weekly storytelling sessions for younger children; and sometimes talks about popular authors for older ones. One daughter was tempted to try the homework club in the 'cool' cafe environment. The other signed up to the teenage reading group after a librarian gave it a glowing review.

It's a good way to make productive use of a spring evening, or a bad-weather day. Be enthusiastic about this literary treasure trove – your joy will rub off.

BOB BARTON

See a musical at home

✳

DAYS that are dark, wet and depressing don't have to be all doom and gloom – forget your troubles, c'mon get happy and sing and dance along to a Hollywood musical in the comfort of your front room! Clear the floor, stick a film in the machine and wait for the kids to take inspiration from the Technicolor feel-good dynamism of, say, *Meet Me in St Louis*, *Mary Poppins*, *The Wizard of Oz* or *Singin' in the Rain*. I defy them to sit still for too long. My kids find it hard to resist splashing about with Gene Kelly, falling about like scarecrows in *The Wizard of Oz* or duetting 'Under the Bamboo Tree', complete with hats and canes like Judy Garland and Margaret O'Brien in *Meet Me in St Louis*.

Like most five- and seven-year-olds, my daughters are obsessed with dressing up – 'I'm Esther!', 'I'm Dorothy' – so encouraging them to scavenge for props and get into character with mad hats, scarves and sparkly shoes is no problem. We don't bother much with CBeebies now – if we're in need of an instant pick-me-up, we just use DVD scene-selection to fast-track to 'The Trolley Song' with Judy, 'Jolly Holiday' with Julie Andrews or 'Make 'Em Laugh' with Donald O'Connor. And off we go again. What a glorious feeling, we're happy again!

JANE RICHARDS

Recreate the cinema at home

※

FORGET family bonding over a jug of gravy, as the advert suggests. Nope, down our way, family night means cinema night. The inspired creation of my son's mate, Louis – who comes from a long line of thespians who don't do anything by halves – cinema night turns your average DVD rental into a full-on 'experience'.

First off, select your film. Ideally this should involve an element of (possibly heated) family debate, but don't overlook films from your own childhood: the likes of *Bugsy Malone* and the original *Willy Wonka & the Chocolate Factory* take on a new light viewed as a parent and make fantastic film-night fodder. (Do resist the temptation to sing along. Aside from embarrassing your children, anyone creating a disturbance may be ejected by the management.)

This being a cinema, you're going to need tickets – so get your enterprising offspring to make and then sell these to you in return for their pocket money – and 'favourite food' snacks. Oh the joy at not being fleeced into paying a tenner for two Fruit Shoots and a bucket of stale, germ-ridden popcorn (Have you seen how kids help themselves to the stuff at the local multi-screen?). Instead try Popz Microwave Popcorn: at around £1.79 for a three-pack, you won't mind so much when they spill the lot on the floor.

Cinema night's also a great incentive for good behaviour. So dust down those star charts and pit your kids against each other. The one with the most stars at the end of the week gets to choose the film, second place the snacks and so on. This is somewhat harder if you've only got one child as you have to throw your own hat into the ring. But if I'm really polite and don't shout too much this week I think I stand a good chance of winning.

Finally, having checked that everyone's been to the loo, it's time for the film to begin. At this point you must, quite literally, turn off the house lights, before giving up your tickets and being ushered to your seat by kids armed with torches.

Now sshhh, cuddle up and enjoy the film. Oh, and don't forget to turn off your mobile.

ABIGAIL FLANAGAN

Try brass rubbing

※

WHEN I was growing up, no school trip was complete without a bit of brass rubbing but when I mentioned the idea to my children they looked at me blankly. The activity that involves placing a sheet of paper over a church brass and rubbing it with wax until an impression appears seems to have fallen from favour, but there are a number of visitor attractions around the UK where you can bring back its shine.

Torre Abbey (www.torre-abbey.org.uk), a medieval monastery in Torquay, reopened in 2008 after a three-year, £6.5m restoration project. This rambling 122-room, sea-front building includes a brass rubbing centre where families can have a go on a collection of 60 replica brasses – the originals were lost during the dissolution of the monasteries. No experience is needed and materials – which include metallic waxes and specialist papers – are provided.

You can also do it at the London Brass Rubbing Centre at St Martin in the Fields Church, just off Trafalgar Square (020 7766 1122) and at the Stratford Brass Rubbing Centre (01789 297671) in Stratford-on-Avon. If your family gets hooked, it's a hobby that could keep you all busy for a while – there are an estimated 8,000 monumental brasses in churches around the UK.

NIKKI SPENCER

Watch some outdoor theatre

※

'IT'S not that different from a normal Saturday night,' says Miranda, aged seven. What can she mean? We are tramping across a field at 7pm, laden with rugs, cushions, fleeces, a picnic and a flask. 'Well, normally we sit and watch a film on the telly and have snacks. Tonight we're watching live telly, and instead of being on the sofa, we're in a garden ...'

Our 'film' is *The Railway Children,* adapted as a live, outdoor show and performed by Heartbreak Productions at Tyntesfield, a National Trust pile outside Bristol. Outdoor theatre may lack subtlety, but it's perfect for kids. The actors run through the picnicking audience, delighting the children, and the stage is a large red train. Miranda was thrilled with the periodic, and effusive, steam emissions from the engine. Best of all, there's no anxiety about keeping little ones quiet and engaged: one child who needed to let off steam, simply did a few cartwheels up the central aisle, without causing anyone any bother.

For Miranda, the highlight was when she joined a crowd of young fans to chat about the play to the actors. And that is something you definitely can't do after you've watched the telly.

Outdoor productions take place across the UK during the summer months – search online for a performance near you. The National Trust run a nationwide programme; see www.nationaltrust.org.uk for details. For Heartbreak's programme, see www.heartproductions.co.uk

JOANNA MOORHEAD

See Shakespeare outside

❈

HAVING twins, I'm very fond of *Twelfth Night*. Richard III is my idea of a stirring, action-packed night out. But until now it has been an adult-only activity. Understandably, my seven-year-old twins aren't that bothered about the great bard. Not even *A Midsummer Night's Dream* will make them sit still and stare at a stage for a couple of hours. But come, gentle night – I've discovered the way to seduce the twins into watching Shakespeare is to see it under the stars. At an outdoor theatre, there's no need for hush.

Noise floats away, and no child, however chatty, is going to be louder than the 747 overhead or the truck reversing up the nearby road. Outdoors, you can also move around easily, so if they get fidgety they can wander off without causing a chorus of tuts.

Search online for an outdoor Shakespeare production near you. For performances in Regent's Park see www.openairtheatre. org. Shakespeare's open air Globe Theatre has an extensive programme in London which also tours nationwide.

DEA BIRKETT

Sing along to a film

※

SING-A-LONG-A *Sound of Music* isn't just about singing, we soon discovered when we arrived at the Prince Charles cinema off Leicester Square in London for a family-friendly showing. It's also about dressing up and our fellow audience members included tribes of Von Trapps in matching curtain-material outfits, a gaggle of girls in white dresses with blue satin sashes, a few nuns, a fairy (no, I didn't remember one in the film either but she looked very cute and even won a prize) and a deer ('doe, a deer', of course).

My two daughters and their friends soon got into the swing of things, belting out 'How Do You Solve a Problem Like Maria?' at the tops of their voices, wielding props from their goody bags at key moments in the film and booing the baroness whenever she appeared.

At the end, in various corners of the foyer, people were changing out of their outfits before leaving. It's clearly one thing to parade in floral frocks and lederhosen in the privacy of a cinema but quite another on a commuter train.

The singalong concept has now spawned a whole range of shows which take place around the UK as well as abroad. Visit www.singalonga.net for a full tour list.

Sing alongs usually take place on the last Friday of every month, but there are extra performances in the school holidays. For details of other family-friendly Sing-a-long-a performances at the Prince Charles cinema, phone 020 7494 3654.

NIKKI SPENCER

Go to the theatre

＊

THE theatre still comes up trumps as a big family event, but it's not cheap. The trick, when you're shelling out on an afternoon's entertainment, is to make sure it goes further than just one afternoon. We themed one summer around a trip to London's Royal Festival Hall to see *The Wizard of Oz*. We read the book and watched the DVD. We dressed up as lions and scarecrows and made scarecrow hats. We even decorated red shoes with sequins to turn them into magic slippers – and finally, we headed to the Royal Festival Hall at the London Southbank Centre for the big day itself: the show.

With the build-up, it could hardly fail to wow us – and wow us it did. To make the most of the show, we went to the matinee performance, and took our towels and swimming costumes along. Afterwards, the fountains outside the Hayward gallery kept the children entertained for another hour or two.

Southbank Centre: www.southbankcentre.co.uk

JOANNA MOORHEAD

Explore classic book locations

※

FOLLOW in the footsteps of Lyra and Will in Philip Pullman's Oxford, play Poohsticks at the original bridge in the 100 Acre Wood (Ashdown Forest, East Sussex), explore the Hampshire landscape of Richard Adams' *Watership Down* – and track down many other children's writers and their characters with a map and interactive website produced by Enjoy England. The map focuses on leading children's authors from Robert Louis Stevenson (*Treasure Island* – Bristol) to Anthony Horowitz (Alex Rider series – London), Rudyard Kipling (*Puck of Pook's Hill*, *The Jungle Book* – East Sussex) to Beatrix Potter (Cumbria) and of course JK Rowling – King's Cross station. On the back of the map and on the excellent website are even more suggestions, by region, of author locations to explore – enough to keep you in days out (and reading) for a year.

The map is free and can be ordered through the website: www.enjoyengland.com/storybook

JULIET RIX

See Corpse Bride

✳

'OH, it's *The Nightmare Before Christmas*,' we cried, as the stop-motion animation spookiness and the Tim Burton gothic wildness began. And so it is, kind of.

The story is from a Russian folk tale. Fish-paste heir Victor is to marry an impoverished aristocratic girl he has never met. Being physically identical (pale grey, with eyeballs bigger than their waists) they bond sensitively over a piano keyboard but are torn asunder when he inadvertently marries the Corpse Bride and is carted off to deadland. Will true love triumph?

Deadland is a lot of fun thanks to a rocking band of hep jazz skeletons who owe much to Cab Calloway, Bob Fosse and Busby Berkeley and quite a lot to the Funnybones books.

Whimsical, however, it ain't. It's strongish stuff, and truly revolting in places: cries of 'Eeewwwwwgh! Minging!' from my juvenile companion were as frequent as hoots of laughter. If your kid can deal with a dripping maggot who lives behind your eye and keeps popping it out to comment on your affairs, then you're on fairly safe ground. But for more sensitive children, there is plenty here to feed their nightmares. Be warned.

LOUISA YOUNG

Corpse Bride (cert PG) is available to buy on DVD, see www.amazon.co.uk

Revisit Godzilla

✳

THEY'VE strolled among dinosaurs in *Jurassic Park*, ducked as alien death-ray-dealing tripods stalked humanity in *The War of the Worlds*, and encountered no end of fantastic creatures in *The Lord of the Rings*. In fact they've taken just about everything state-of-the-art computer-generated cinema trickery can throw at them, so why on earth should my children want to watch a naff Japanese horror movie from 1954 featuring a giant lizard that's clearly being played by a little bloke in a rubber suit?

Ishiro Honda's marvellous original is as much a rumination on the evil of nuclear war as a horror movie. The US version excised all that and gave us instead an all-American hero called Raymond Burr, who was so emotionless he looked like he was being played by a little bloke in a rubber Raymond Burr suit.

But the kids won't care about all that. All they need to know is that Godzilla is the true king of the screen monsters. One blast of his fiery breath would turn King Kong into a heap of smouldering ashes. This is a 50-metres-tall, city-trashing mountain of sheer terror. Look, children, Godzilla comes this way! Flee for your life! Aiiiiiiyyeeeee!!

PAUL HOWLETT

Godzilla [1954] (cert PG) is available to buy on DVD, see www.amazon.co.uk

Enjoy Jane Austen

✳

Eᴸᴵɴᴏʀ, 11, a huge fan of Keira Knightley, was so keen to see *Pride and Prejudice* that she was knocking on the cinema door the day it was released. The mummies tried their best to go along too, but we were gently rebuffed ('Are you mad? We don't want old people with us.') But – oh miracle – when she came home enthusing about the film, astonishingly, she consented to me reading the first few pages of the book itself to her. It was an immediate hit, helped by various parallels between us and the Bennets. Not only were they a family with all girls (though just four in our case, not five), but they were, like us, blessed with an acerbic father.

Our own Mr Bennet, when informed of Elinor's new-found love of Jane Austen, began to make unflattering comparisons between the real and fictional wife. Well, I hope I'm not foisting Austen on my daughter in quite the way Mrs B foisted suitors onto her offspring, but I admit that I am delighting in her growing penchant for an author I approve of hugely. Next weekend, I'm seizing the moment and we're off to Hampshire to visit Chawton, Austen's final home: like Mrs B, once I sniff a daughter's enthusiasm for something improving, I'm not letting go.

For information on Chawton, call 01420 83262 or visit www.jane-austens-house-museum.org.uk.

JOANNA MOORHEAD

Pride and Prejudice (cert U), is available to buy on DVD, see www.amazon.co.uk

———

117

See Oliver Twist

✳

ROMAN Polanski? Ben Kingsley? And Bill Sykes? I'm terrified already. I've seen *Repulsion*. I've seen *Sexy Beast*. This does not, frankly, sound like a PG film. But PG is the certificate borne by Polanski's version of Oliver Twist, so off I went, with a 12-year-old for guidance, to see how scary it actually is. The answer is: quite, actually. It's magnificently traditional, foggy and muddy with rats underfoot, sooty Victorian clothing and lots of looming out of the shadows. I start crying as soon as Oliver asks for more. The 12-year-old bears up much better but by the time Oliver's feet are bleeding and he faints in the road, let alone when Sykes beats Nancy to death, tries to murder the big ugly dog ('But it's a dog! Poor dog!' cries the 12-year-old) and accidentally hangs himself by moonlight on a black and slippery rooftop, she too is mildly agog. At the end she was quite firm.

'Eight-year-olds should see this because it's very good,' she declared, 'but not without a hand to hold. It should be PG.' Other scary things: Ben Kingsley (Fagin) looked exactly like Ron Moody; Jamie Foreman (Sykes) looked exactly like Oliver Reed; Mark Strong, usually so butch and handsome, was a degenerate psycho fop with curly, wispy orange hair.

LOUISA YOUNG

Oliver Twist (cert PG) is available to buy on DVD, see www.amazon.co.uk

See Wallace & Gromit

✳

I'VE been waiting for a suitable film to take my three-year-old son to for a while now. At Postman Pat earlier this year, he was clearly not ready for the noise or the dark – though he occasionally peered through the doors at the back. But at last I think I have found the ideal film in the brilliant *Wallace & Gromit: The Curse of the Were-Rabbit*, our plasticine pals' first feature-length outing.

As the Giant Vegetable Competition nears, our heroes are busy capturing the rabbits who are wreaking havoc in the town's back gardens. The sudden appearance of a giant, seemingly unstoppable veg-seeking rabbit seems to have something to do with Wallace's latest invention, the Mind-Manipulation-O-Matic.

As you'd expect of an Aardman animation, you'll enjoy spotting a treasure trove of detail, from Wallace and Gromit's Smug fridge, to the cheese-obsessed Wallace's bookshelf (East of Edam, Fromage to Eternity, etc) and flawless sight gags.

Children will love the cutesy rabbits, beguiling gadgets and the frenetic pace, while adults can enjoy the film references, cheesy double entendres and Helena Bonham Carter's toothy toff. Now, to prime my son with the three previous Wallace and Gromit adventures on DVD just to make sure...

CHRIS HALL

Wallace & Gromit: The Curse of the Were-Rabbit (cert U), is available to buy on DVD, see www.amazon.co.uk

——•——

Teach your children air guitar

✳

IT'S raining. Your kids are bored. Why not introduce them to a hobby they can be good at instantly and that will keep them occupied for hours, even years? Simply dust off your old air guitar (it must be somewhere – look in the attic), put on AC/DC or Eric Clapton and boogie on down. Kids will love the windmill arm movements and the cool facial expressions (tell them to imagine they've just swallowed some medicine...) Before bed they will be ready to play their first air gig.

Later, you can relax and watch *Newsnight,* radiant in the knowledge that you could have lit within your little ones the blue touchpaper that ignites a whole air musical career! First violin in an air symphony orchestra, perhaps, or – the holy grail of air music – a top job as an air composer! The only limit is their imagination.

STEVEN APPLEBY

Better Living Through Air Guitar by Steven Appleby and George Mole is published by Portrait Books.

120

Make a book box

✳

MY children love playing with the toys I had as a child. They've taken my Tiny Tears and threadbare teddies to their hearts, and worn my wooden doll's pram into the ground. But my books are my real treasures. So putting them all in a special chest is a good way of keeping them that way – to be brought out under strict supervision on rainy days. Of course, making the chest is a good rainy-day activity in itself. Find a big cardboard box, get out the poster paints, scissors, glue and glittery bits – and get decorating. The treasures themselves – dog-eared, musty-smelling and invariably falling apart at the seams – have their own special air of mystery and fragility and provide endless talking points. My kids really love seeing the inscriptions on the inside page – my childish scrawl painstakingly spelling out my full name; they love that I felt-tipped in most of the black and white illustrations ('Was your mummy cross with you?!') and are thrilled to see the inscription in my beautiful hard-back, illustrated edition of *The Secret Garden*, 'To my dear great-niece on her ninth birthday with love from Great Aunt Edith'. My girls are amazed that I was reading the same books as them when I was a child – Roald Dahl's *Fantastic Mr Fox*, Dorothy Edwards' *My Naughty Little Sister* and EB White's *Charlotte's Web*. Next up, Tove Jansson's *Finn Family Moomintroll* and Noel Streatfield's *Ballet Shoes* – that is, if we can make out the words through the felt-tip marks.

JANE RICHARDS

Put on your own puppet show

'TWAS a chilly November evening, when all we wanted to do was sit by the fire and make up stories. The moon that night was full and shone through our window, and against the clear sky it looked huge. My son was convinced it was coming down to earth. And so our puppet-show script began. 'Script' makes it sound very grand – it was really just a list of events on a piece of paper – but this was enough, we could ad-lib the rest as the show began.

A shadow puppet show is really easy to set up, and very atmospheric. You can make the puppets by moving your hand into different shapes against a wall, or you can cut puppets out of cardboard with limbs and wings that you can move around using paper fasteners. We use a bit of both techniques, and cut up cereal boxes for some of the puppets, keeping the outline simple.

You can also make a simple theatre by cutting one side off a large cereal box. Make a large hole in the front of it, and then staple a bit of white fabric across the hole to form the screen. Set up a lamp to light the screen from behind, hold your puppets up to the back of the screen, turn off all the other lights, and let the play begin.

MELISSA VIGUIER

Turn cardboard into theatre

✳

A good big box is a marvellous thing because children love them. After Christmas is particularly good because you've got all those boxes from the large presents Santa brings lying around. We cut a hole in one side and rigged up a makeshift curtain with a piece of material and some string, and the box became an all-in-one theatre, shop, castle and log cabin.

The box lives folded up in the attic, ready for dark afternoons in the holidays. However bored and fractious the kids are they cheer up when we drag the battered cardboard down the ladder. A piece of tape to square it up and a running repair to the curtain is all it takes and, hey presto!

Cushions are dragged in. Dolls are found. A tea party becomes a cake sale, which evolves into a puppet show.

The children are happy inside their box. We're happy outside, watching a chaotic drama about rabbits.

JAMES RUSSELL

Days of discovery

Scientific research and other investigations

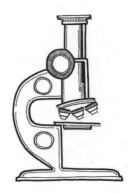

Predict the weather

✳

WEATHER is a national obsession in the UK, particularly in the months most susceptible to climatic extremes. Set up as forecasters with some homemade equipment and you may be amazed by your accuracy.

Start by making a barometer to measure pressure changes and the likelihood of rain, with an empty jam jar and clear wine bottle. Place the wine bottle upside down in the jar and pour in enough water to just cover the bottle neck. Remove the bottle and pour the water into it. Put the jar over the top of the bottle and, holding both together, turn them upside down. Mark the water level and the barometer is ready. When the level drops it means pressure is also dropping and rain may be imminent. Ideally, set it up on a low-pressure (rainy) day.

Complete your forecast by observing the wind direction with the aid of thin strips of newspaper attached to a stick or branch. Use a compass to get your bearings. The saying 'every wind has its weather' is often true. In the UK, wind from the west often brings rain and from the north-east plunging temperatures and snow.

BOB BARTON

Discover the basics of botany

✳

EXPLAINING how plants work can be difficult at the best of times. Luckily, there is one trick that you can use to simply show children the basics of botany. Take a few sticks of celery, trim the root ends, and place them in 100ml of coloured water. Within a few hours, the leaves will start to change colour. Eventually the stems will also take on the colour. The longer they are left in the water, the more they will take up. You can even produce 'rainbow celery' by partially slicing one large stick twice lengthways to create three conjoined sticks. Place each of the three sticks into water containing a different colour. Kids love to predict which colours will attain uptake most rapidly. Don't spoil their fun by telling them that it is always the dark ones.

VINCENT REID

Start the fungus wars

✳

PUT a piece of soggy bread in an old ice-cream tub, seal it and keep it somewhere warm. Every day, changes in growth of the various moulds can be seen. Children can draw the main fungi patterns on a piece of paper and track growth changes over time. They can see how one fungus grows and dies when its preferred food source runs out, only to be replaced by another type better suited to the environment.

Territory wars between different fungi can be fun: you can even place bets on which side will win. If you're lucky, one fungus will parasitically eat another. After 10 days, some impressive types of mould can be seen, from silky-grey curly hairs to black sticky tendrils. The range of colours are often astonishing, from black, brown and dark orange to bright green and pastel blue.

If your kids really like it, you can even give it a name. Ours was the Forest of Dean, later becoming just Dean. But being on a first-name basis is not such a good thing when it's time to bin your jungle. Tears from younger ecologists will inevitably flow.

VINCENT REID

Become a pharologist

*

THE study of signal lights and lighthouses is called pharology. Princess Anne is said to be a pharologist. She has made pilgrimages to around 80 lighthouses as patron of the Northern Lighthouse Board, which is responsible for the upkeep of all the lighthouses around Scotland and the Isle of Man, and is also said to have made private expeditions to other more remote lighthouses.

So where does the term pharolgy come from? It is taken from Pharos, the huge marble lighthouse built off the coast of Alexandria in the third century BC. For centuries one of the tallest man-made structures on earth, the Pharos lighthouse was identified as one of the ancient seven wonders of the world. (The other six included the Great Pyramid and the Colossus of Rhodes). Early lighthouses used fires of wood or charcoal. The oldest lighthouse in this country is in the grounds of Dover Castle. You can, alas, no longer become a lighthouse keeper in the UK: the last lighthouse was automated in 1998. But you can join the many enthusiasts of all ages who visit and stay at lighthouses.

For general information about lighthouses, go to the Association of Lighthouse Keepers' website (www.alk.org.uk) and for a list of lighthouse accommodation see Trinity House, the General Lighthouse Authority, at www.trinityhouse.co.uk

IAN SANSOM

Make a wind farm

※

To make your own wind farm you'll need 20 to 40 pinwheel windmills depending on the size of your garden. Luckily, they usually come in packs of five at your local supermarket.

First, marshal your children and give them an equal number of windmills. After showing them how to plant one, let them loose.

Once your wind farm has been set up, the fun really begins. This is where you and the kids can argue about why some sites are better than others. In a matter of a few minutes you can touch on topics as diverse as microclimates, energy transfer, speed and power as well as capture rates, rotation speeds and the need to align the windmill in the direction of the wind. All of this can be done by seeing which ones are spinning the fastest and which the slowest.

Wind farms are also very successful activities for party events, particularly when there is a prize for the child whose windmill rotates the fastest. As everyone at the party should ideally get a prize, you can also invent awards such as 'foolish location, but most likely to get planning consent'.

The children won't even notice that you have taught them most of the GCSE syllabus for physics. Best of all, you will now know where to place your home turbine should you ever wish to produce your own electricity.

www.gcse.com/physics.htm and www.physicsclassroom.com are good general physics websites; the British Wind Energy Association is at www.bwea.com

VINCENT REID

Make a volcano in the kitchen

✳

TURN your kitchen into a science lab and amaze the children, using ingredients from the cupboard. Start by making a volcano. Use a small plastic cup with about a third cut off at the top, this will be the caldera. Around the cup, Sellotape a cone of cardboard to create a mountain, keeping the cup open at the top. Decorate or colour the cardboard, if you wish, to resemble a mountain. To the cup add a tablespoon of baking powder or bicarbonate of soda and a few drops of food colouring (green or red are good) and mix to a paste. To set off the volcano pour on some vinegar, a couple of tablespoons should do, and wait for the reaction.

Within seconds you will have coloured frothy lava spilling down the mountainside. The science bit: vinegar is an acid and it reacts with the soda, an alkali, to produce a salt. While the reaction is taking place you get froth (carbon dioxide) and a little heat.

It's a good idea to protect the table or do this in the garden.

JOANN LEEDING

Find the best place for an echo

✳

WE all know the powerful, Elvis-type voice that's possible when we're singing in the bath, but we've been having more fun with echoes. On a stroll along the Thames in Berkshire recently, we tried singing and shouting under the railway bridge at Maidenhead. We had heard that this part of Brunel's bridge (painted by Turner in *Rain, Steam and Speed*), is known as the Sounding Arch, but were astounded by the strength of the echo that bounced back, reverberating around the smooth brickwork.

Since then we've found other good echoes and have even recorded some on a mobile phone. Before the digital age, music recording engineers knew that places such as stairwells, bathrooms and large empty halls made impromptu echo chambers. Set yourself a challenge to experiment and find the best locations. Hard surfaces and high ceilings: glass, concrete, tile and bare plaster are ideal.

The best results occur when there's nothing soft, such as trees or curtain fabric, to absorb any noise. Then the sound waves just keep bouncing backwards and forwards. Have a go with household and garden objects too – try large empty cans, metal drums or buckets. Maybe you are lucky enough to live near a canal tunnel, pedestrian underpass or even a cavern.

BOB BARTON

Make gooey slime

✳

CHILDREN love making revolting stuff and it doesn't get much more disgusting than this formula for truly gooey slime courtesy of science and engineering website noisemakers.org.uk (they also have lots of ideas for other experiments you can do at home). For the slime, you need 5g of borax, a detergent salt available from hardware shops or pharmacies, which you need to make into a solution with 100ml of water.

In a bowl, mix a few drops of food colouring (blue and green are good for maximum impact) in a quarter of a cup of water, then gradually stir in about a quarter of a cup of PVA glue. When it's all mixed in, slowly pour in the borax solution (the more you use the stickier it gets), stirring continuously, and watch the slime bubble up before your very eyes. Everyone will want to roll up their sleeves and play with the stuff although the experiment does come with a warning – do not eat this or feed it to your cat/dog/younger siblings!

The site also has a recipe for Mentos-Coke Fountains, where you put a whole packet of mints into a large bottle of fizzy drink and then stand well back. Whatever you do though, do not try this indoors as it makes a very sticky mess. And I mean very.

NIKKI SPENCER

Investigate your snacks

✳

THIS experiment can show just how much fat there is in a lot of snacks compared with apples, which contain no fat. The principle is that at 100C, fats are liquid and will float on water.

What you need: an apple; a chopping board and knife; a saucepan; water; a chocolate bar, packet of crisps or other fatty snack.

What to do: chop your apple into small pieces and put it into a pan of boiling water. Simmer for a few minutes – this will make any fat content melt and rise to the top. You should see that there is virtually nothing there. Repeat the experiment with your fatty snack, and you will see a scummy, gloopy layer rise to the surface. Imagine that in your stomach!

The science: fat is made up of molecules containing long chains, which do not interact well with water. When heated so that they liquefy, they will rise to the surface of the water because not only will they not mix with the water but they are less dense than water, too.

HELEN BOND

Make a black apple

❋

HAVE you ever thought about why things are coloured? This experiment will show you how different colours or wavelengths of light make objects appear differently.

What you need: one red apple and one green apple; a small torch; a pair of red/green 3D specs or some red and green film from a photographic shop; Blu-Tack (or similar).

What to do: attach the green film to the front of the torch, using the Blu-Tack.

You should make sure that no light seeps around the edges, ie all the light coming from the torch should be green with no chinks of white light. Take your coloured torch and the apples into a very dark room and shine the torch on them. Can you tell which is which? Which one appears more pale?

Now repeat the experiment but use the red film to make your torch produce red light. Now which apple appears more pale? Are you surprised? This experiment is non-destructive so you can now eat the apples!

How it works: white light is made up of light of all wavelengths or colours. Red things appear red because they reflect the red part of the light and absorb all the other colours. Similarly, green things reflect green light and absorb all the other colours.

When you put the red film on your torch and shine it at a red apple you can see the reflected light and it appears pale. But when you shine red light on a green apple, the red light is absorbed and it appears dark. The opposite is true for green light.

HELEN BOND

—•—

Drop an apple for science

✻

HAVE you ever wondered why things fall at different speeds? This simple experiment shows a surprising result first noticed more than 300 years ago.

What you need: an apple and a sheet of paper.

What to do: hold the apple and the paper at the same height from the ground and release them simultaneously. This is best done over a soft surface, such as a thick carpet, to avoid damaging your apple.

Which hits the ground first? You probably weren't too surprised by the result. Now scrunch the paper into a round ball about the same size as the apple. Repeat the experiment. Does the apple still beat the paper to the ground? Do it a few more times to convince yourself of the result.

Finally, brush off your apple and eat it while thinking about the explanation ...

The science: the only thing that makes the paper reach the ground more slowly than the apple is the extra air resistance caused by its high surface area. As soon as you make the paper into a ball the same size as the apple, they fall at exactly the same rate and hit the ground together.

Why? Well, the apple, as the object with the greater mass, has a larger gravitational force attracting it to the ground. However, this is exactly cancelled by the fact that it has more inertia. In other words, its extra mass means that it takes more 'oomph' to get it moving.

As it turns out, any object accelerates towards the ground at the same rate when other factors, such as air resistance, are removed. This was first demonstrated by Galileo in the 17th century and studied in more detail by Isaac Newton. A variation of the experiment was shown beautifully during the Apollo 15 trip to the moon, when the astronaut David Scott was filmed dropping a hammer and a feather together. There is no air on the moon, so no air resistance, so they both hit the ground at the same time.

HELEN BOND

Do an energy audit

✳

JUST as Nell, seven, and her friend Clara, six, start to bicker the morning after a sleepover, I intervene with a new game – the energy audit. First we make a kit of tape measure, notebook, pen and super-sized matches. Then we start our energy audit looking for draughts, flimsy window coverings, gappy floorboards and absent insulation. My role is to ensure the girls know that it costs money to heat space. 'Money that could be spent on sweets instead,' I say shamelessly. Their mission is to find all the ways heat escapes from the house. We light a match by the cellar door: both flame and smoke go straight up. 'That means it's well draught-proofed,' I bluff, smugly. But at the back door the smoke angles off at 90 degrees, indicating a major draught. The front door is as bad. Nell uses her fingers to locate the air stream, then measures the gaps so that I can fit a draught excluder.

In the sitting room I challenge my auditors to find the place where most heat escapes, hinting that it is big enough for a child to hide in. They look behind the sofa for a long time, ignoring the fireplace. When they eventually guess the spot we decide a chimney balloon is needed to lock the heat in.

When the doorbell rings, it is noticeable how quickly our visitor says goodbye – hopefully she's just keen to do an energy audit for her mum. For more ways to be green go to the Centre for Alternative Technology's website (cat.org.uk/information/howgreen.tmpl)

NICOLA BAIRD

How Can I Stop Climate Change? by Helen Burley and Chris Haslam is published by Collins.

Bottle the colours of autumn

✳

EVERYBODY knows autumn is pretty, but how many know that this is largely due to plant excrement? As daylight hours decrease, the chlorophyll (the green bit of the leaf that converts sunlight into energy) dissolves, revealing colours that have always been there, often the products of waste.

You can capture all of these colours relatively easily. Collect different-coloured leaves, including one still green such as laurel, nettle or fresh spinach from the supermarket. Next, you will need surgical spirit, or acetone, some small jars, a large flat dish, hot water and coffee filter papers (bleached).

Cut up the leaves into tiny pieces, then grind them with a mortar and pestle. Pour each colour into its own jar, cover with a few millimetres of surgical spirit or acetone and place the jars in the dish and pour in some very hot water. This may need to be topped up to keep it heated for at least half an hour.

Remove jars from the heat, take the lids off and dip a strip of filter paper into each one, which should be left for at least half an hour. The theory is that the alcohol rises up the paper through capillary action, pulling up pigment from the solution. As it evaporates, different colours travel different distances. If you are lucky, the paper dries to reveal a good spread of colours.

BENJAMIN MEE

Map sun spots

※

WHEN people think about astronomy, they usually picture stars at night. But you can just as safely investigate the sun during the day. Before embarking on this activity, children should be reminded that looking directly at the sun can seriously damage eyesight. All you will need are: a pencil, a piece of white paper (and something to hold it in position for an extended period of time, such as a music stand) and binoculars or a telescope. Position your paper below the small lens of your instrument. Then project the sunlight on to the paper. Once focused, this will show an image of the sun – a bright circle of light. Inside the circle, you will be able to see small dark spots – these are sunspots. Mark their location on the paper.

When you return later in the day you will find that the spots have moved. By mapping the sunspots over a period of time you can determine the axis of the sun's rotation. Throughout the day you can also check to see whether the sun appears to change shape. It does this near sunrise and sunset when the earth's atmosphere distorts its shape. And have a book on astronomy handy to help with your explanation that each small spot is, in fact, an image of a magnetic storm that is bigger than the Earth.

Check out the solar section of the British Astronomical Association's website (www.britastro.org/solar/index.php?style=new) and general astronomy website www.astronomyforbeginners. com

VINCENT REID

Go stargazing

※

'HAVE you run up the hill?' asks the attendant, as my husband, son and I arrive, gasping, at the Royal Observatory's Peter Harrison Planetarium with seconds to spare.

Shattered, we fall into the huge, comfy seats just as the lights go down and the planetarium's dome retracts to reveal a computerised night sky. The Sky Tonight is a live show, so we're guided to constellations, planets, cosmic gas clouds and more by a Royal Observatory astronomer. Her fascinating commentary takes in both science and mythology as we explore the galaxies; visiting planets we can see with the naked eye and way beyond. The graphics are superb and Joe, my eight-year-old, is spellbound. It's an incredible journey for a small boy to take in an afternoon. 'I feel really, really small,' says Joe, as the lights come back on. 'Me too,' I say. 'Me too.'

For the Royal Observatory Greenwich, go to www.nmm. ac.uk (0870 781 5167). There are planetariums all over the country with shows for junior stargazers. To find your nearest, log on to planetaria.org.uk

ABIGAIL FLANAGAN

Explore aerodynamics

※

THE aviation industry is in the process of change. A new generation of aeroplanes is emerging. Your budding engineers may be the inventors of tomorrow if they understand aerodynamics today. The first thing to do is find a small stone, and get the kids to see if it will float on air. This should then be compared with the descent of a feather. After the laws of gravity have been implicitly understood, the paper-dart-making can begin.

There are no rules to making darts, with the exception that it should have a definable nose.

Then, attach some string to the nose. You can now assess the dart's aerodynamic capability. Hold the string and arc your hand up and down. If your dart wafts on air, then you are on the right track. It your dart dangles from your string like a conker, you need to start again. Serious engineers can test their designs in a homemade wind tunnel, which can be either a desk fan on a low setting or the vacuum cleaner with the reverse function activated.

Generally, if your creation can ride on the wind rather than spinning around on the end of your string, then you have a winner. But adults should be warned: the quest for the perfect dart can take a lifetime.

VINCENT REID

143

Create a cloud

✳

THE two 11-year-olds looked suspicious. They'd bemoaned the likely lack of snow at Christmas so I'd claimed I could make a snow cloud in a jar. I'd over-promised – but making a cloud was within my compass so hopefully they would be so impressed with the miniature nimbus everyone would forget the bit about snow.

Here's how to do it. Get a glass jar, a small, chilled, metal dish and some ice. Pour some hot water into the jar and place the dish, complete with ice, on top. Now you should start to see what looks like a cloud forming at the top of the jar. Here's the science bit: clouds form when warm, moist air like that trapped in the jar is cooled – hence the ice. In the real world, as warm air rises it expands and cools, eventually becoming saturated and condensing into the tiny water droplets that form clouds.

Back to the mini-cloud factory – if you want to spice things up, take off the dish and hold a lit match briefly in the jar before replacing your icy lid. Now shake the jar and things become cloudier than an overcast day in winter. Not sure about the science – something about smoke and water particles mixing – but the results are ace.

'Wow! That's wicked.' Bingo, they were impressed. 'What about the snow?' Bah!

ANTONY JONES

144

Days outdoors

Having fun in the fresh air

Let them eat mud

※

ACCORDING to a recent survey (of five of my friends), the final weekend of January is when you're most likely to admit defeat in the entertaining-the-kids stakes. The combination of short days, foul weather and offspring buzzing like fridges can quickly drive you towards some hateful indoor adventure playground.

So fight back. Forget the driving sleet and lack of daylight: pull on your wellies, wrap up warm, head for your nearest patch of green and promise yourself that you will not utter the words 'Stay out of those puddles'.

Because kids don't need 9m-high play frames to have fun. They just need mud and water – and parents who won't scream at them if they get really, really dirty. Remember how much fun you had making mud pies as a kid? Well nowt's changed.

Kids need the chance to let off steam and make a mess – especially when it involves things that are usually discouraged. There doesn't have to be any focus – although mud monsters make a good alternative to snowmen – the most important thing is that they can just play for enjoyment's sake and let their innate curiosity run wild.

Yes, they'll get filthy (bring a change of clothes or put bin bags over the car seats), and yes they'll get cold but that's what warm baths and soap are for. An hour outside in the mud and fresh air is worth a lifetime in play-frame purgatory. And believe me, as someone who once had to dive head-first into a ball pond to retrieve a mobile phone, mud's the far cleaner of the two.

ABIGAIL FLANAGAN

Take a walk along a river

✳

THERE's a dullness, a grimness about an English January that makes it all too tempting to sit huddled around the television rather than to brave the mud and the rain. But that just makes life duller and grimmer. It's true that not all of us have glorious winter landscapes to yomp across, but with a little research, even the most landlocked city dweller can usually find a stretch of river or canal to explore, and there's nothing like running water to wash the glums away.

First, get your child involved in finding the waterway by looking on a map, or better still on Google Earth. Then prepare your 'rations', wrap up and set off.

The thing about rivers is that they never stay still. The trees might be skeletal, but the wildlife and vegetation is as varied in January as at any other time of year. Take a bag of bread crusts and every duck, gull or goose for miles will be at your feet in minutes. Then try naming them all.

For small children, their different behaviours – timid, aggressive, downright pushy – means that they soon develop characters. Wherever there are characters, there are bound to be stories, and a good story can keep a child going for ages.

In some ways, particularly in winter, canals are even better than rivers, especially those tangly industrial ones with ancient cranes sticking out of sinister abandoned warehouses. The trick here is to imagine a crime (preferably a murder) and follow the 'clues' offered by the bits of litter you will find along any urban towpath: an old shoe, a bit of rag, an empty bottle – anything can be enlisted in the unfolding mystery. The last

time we played this game, we even found the murder weapon –
a pair of pristine secateurs which my daughter spotted under
a bush and which have been in use ever since.

As your children get older, your trips can get more ambitious
– both on foot, or even better, on bicycle. In east London, where
I live, it's astonishing how quickly the riverscape changes from
industrial to rural and back again. You can mark the turning-
point with lunch at any number of waterside pubs.

CLAIRE ARMITSTEAD

Go stone skimming

✳

WINTER: stone-skimming season. First, find your beach,
or a pond, or a lake. Any large flat surface of water will
do. Second, find your stone. A spherical stone won't work. The
stone must be flat and it should be roundish.

The secret to stone skimming is spin and tilt. In order for
it to move forward across the surface of the water, the stone
must be spinning. In order for it to bounce across the surface
of the water the stone must be tilted.

The leading edge of the stone must be slightly higher than
the trailing edge. If the leading edge hits the water first the
stone will sink. If the trailing edge hits the water first, the
stone will skip gracefully on the surface and then spin further
forwards, and then skip on the surface again, and again, and
again, until the stone stops spinning, and sinks – and then
you have to find another stone.

IAN SANSOM

Row, row, row your boat

✳

FOR my daughter's eighth birthday party we took a gang of kids to the uncharted waters of Finsbury Park boating lake in north London. OK, it's not Cowes, but even this inept oarsman could look like an impressive dad as he manfully rowed around the lake, while Mum looked uncannily like Ellen McArthur, minus the flares of course, for party health-and-safety reasons.

The children were clipped into yellow life jackets and then we all clambered on board four boats with pirate insignia and England flags painted on them.

We veered toward the island in the middle of the lake. Luckily, the three excited kids in my boat didn't notice how uncoordinated my strokes were and soon I discovered previously hidden nautical instincts. 'Hard to port Miss Lola – Klingons on the starboard bow!'

Watch your kids dangle a leg in the water and wonder if it's quite safe; feel the boat dip dangerously as they lurch out the side trying to retrieve a mangy duck feather floating in the water; row too close to protected birds' nests on the island; molest moorhens and geese; clunk into other boats and push yourself off with an oar. Admire the semi-submerged park bench; try to avoid colliding with that overhanging branch; head for the two spurting mid-lake fountains; let the kids row, taking one oar each (an either oar situation?) and watch as they rotate in a circle; and annoy the attendant on the bank by exceeding your half-hour allocation because you want to perfect your three-point aquatic turn in front of admiring eight-year-olds.

PETE MAY

Walk behind a waterfall

※

WOULDN'T it be good to sample an April shower without getting wet? One of the most exhilarating ways to do so is by walking behind a waterfall. Spring is an ideal time as rivers are in full spate.

This isn't something you can do at any waterfall, though. Water and rocks are a dangerous combination, so use an advertised trail. One of our favourites is the Ingleton Waterfalls trail in the Yorkshire Dales, on the A65 Skipton to Kendal road. Its highlight is Thornton Force, a 15m-high fall where you can experience water thundering down in front of you. Make sure children are supervised and equipped with wellies or walking boots. Allow three hours.

Another walk-behind waterfall is Ashgill Force in Cumbria, which crashes over a sheer limestone cliff, past a natural terrace where you can wonder at the curtain of water powering past. It's on the B6277 south of Garrigill near Alston and the drive there is part of the fun — a scenic road over the Pennines, past former lead mines.

There is another example — in a city centre. The water feature in Derby's Market Place is officially a public artwork, but for the children who step behind the rushing torrent (don't worry, it is allowed), it's a scene from Peter Pan. Passing shoppers are used to hearing woops of delight from its shadows.

The Ingleton Waterfalls trail: www.ingletonwaterfallswalk. co.uk

BOB BARTON

———•———

Build a den

✳

GROWING up on a farm in Devon, my three brothers and I regularly built dens out of whatever we could lay our hands on, including asbestos sheeting and clumps of bracken (both of which have been subject to health scares in more recent times but, hey, we are all still here to tell the tale!) and even with the 21st-century distractions of PSPs and MySpace, children still want to follow in the footsteps of the survival expert Ray Mears. Only a few days ago, a friend popped round to raid my shed for anything her 12-year-old son could use to construct a den at the bottom of their garden.

There are lots of den building events around the country including sessions for five- to 12-year-olds at Beechenhurst Lodge in the Forest of Dean (01594 833057) and for families deep in Hamsterley Forest in County Durham (01388 488312) in April, May and August.

In Dalby Forest, Yorkshire (01751 472771), seven- to 11-year-olds can learn how to make use of the woodland surroundings on a Bushcraft Day Camp, while plenty of father-and-child bonding goes on in Chopwell Woodland Park near Gateshead (01388 488312) on their Dad's Day Den Building event.

Of course, the proof of a good den is that it must protect you from the elements, so once the building work is finished a bucket of water is thrown over your handiwork. The ultimate test is whether you are prepared to stay inside while this is done!

Booking is essential for all events. Visit www.forestry.gov.uk for more details – including dates and prices – and for den-building tips.

NIKKI SPENCER

Go creative beachcombing

✳

W E'VE spent hours wandering along beaches picking up unusual objects washed ashore. Rather than storing and forgetting about our finds we make use of them. Bits of tide-washed driftwood and twisted metal become art when placed among the geraniums in our flower tubs. Surf-smoothed coloured sea glass is ideal for candle-dish decoration. Colourful odds and ends of rope and fishing net floats give a nautical twist to our patio. The children put their collection of shells on our gravelled front garden, making an instant beach, which earned compliments from passersby.

Our London walks along the Thames at low tide have resulted in a fledgling collection of 18th and 19th-century clay-pipe fragments. (Wear wellies and old clothes, it can be muddy.) Though broken, these milk-white objects are surprisingly delicate and one lucky pipe find included a decorated bowl in the shape of a lady's head. When displayed on a patch of velvet, they really stand out and our girls love describing how each was found, speculating over who may have used them.

Readers may find other themes running through their flotsam and jetsam finds. Do your bit for the environment, too, by collecting objects such as plastic bottles and wire, that can injure or kill marine life.

BOB BARTON

Make a bow and arrow

✳

'You want me to make a bow and arrow?' 'Yes,' said my nine-year-old mischievously. 'Like the one Robin Hood uses.'

My first attempts were woeful – it was string tied to bowish-shaped wood, but for all its effectiveness it might as well have been a cucumber and a strand of cooked spaghetti. Google would help, surely? Not at first.

Purists advocate finding a piece of springy green yew tree ... and leaving it to dry for a year! Other options involved a grasp of drilling beyond my modest reach. Cripes, why didn't he ask me to make a Transformer out of an old egg box?

Then I find a work of genius: take three or four strips of flat wood, about 4cm wide, in decreasing lengths; put them on top of each other and tape together at the centre. Attach string to each end and bend the bow ensuring the shorter strips of wood are on the inside. Arrows are easier still – get some bamboo, stick on some paper flights at one end and a blob of Blu-Tack on the other to avoid injury, tell young Robin not to point it at any living thing, and – bullseye!

ANTONY JONES

Take some underwater snaps

※

MY most recent memory of using an underwater camera was 20 years ago in Florida. It was big and clunky and, even in those crisp blue waters, the images were murky blotches. Camera technology has improved since then, and if you're packing for a beach or pool holiday take an underwater disposable camera with you. They are fantastic. The kids zoom around pulling faces – it's still a novelty being photographed floating two feet underwater with mermaid's hair and floppy limbs. Underwater cameras are great for snorkellers too – in clear waters you can catch beautiful fish on film.

They're also cheap. You can buy one online from about £8. A small price to pay to turn your son into Marine Boy and your daughter into Neptina.

JANE PHILLIMORE

Have a back-garden adventure

✳

HERE'S how to have an adventure without leaving your own back garden. Pick a summer night, check the forecast for rain, get outside and sleep under the stars. A sleeping bag and ground sheet are the only must-haves, though wimps like me will think of a host of other necessities including pillows, water bottle and insect repellent.

Lying back in our family nest, we marvelled at the sheer hugeness of the star-filled sky above. We felt insignificantly small, yet safe and warm together. We talked about space, light years, infinity, and aliens. Our focus came right back down to earth when Daniel heard something scuttling along the edge of the bushes, and we picked out the shape of a hedgehog hunting out bugs and slugs for supper.

Some home truths about sleeping under the stars: make sure everyone goes to the loo before they snuggle into their sleeping bags, accept that no one's really going to get much sleep, and when you wake up and discover everything's soaking wet, understand that a bit of dew never hurt anyone.

LESLEY CARR

Make a raft

❋

'LAND Ahoy' called the two small boys who were galloping along the banks of the muddy lagoon. They were heading for the minuscule beach that their rafts were just about to reach. It was a fine day, and we had spent the last couple of hours building tiny rafts out of flotsam and jetsam and then chasing them as they sailed away. We began by tying together a bundle of small twigs with an unravelled thread from my coat. This formed the base of the raft upon which those merry little sailors squeezed a dandelion in full flower.

Launched from the swans' pontoon, that little raft glided along and captivated us as we followed it along its journey past the treacherous rocks made from dragon's teeth through the doldrums, and countless battles with swans and other wildfowl. It was quite a journey. No wonder we now regularly go to the pond and see what we can make a raft with. Our most successful design so far has been made by poking a feather into a wormhole in a bit of driftwood – it looks like a prehistoric surfboard for a mouse, but goes like a rocket!

MELISSA VIGUIER

Spot a shooting star

✳

IF you've got the time and the patience, it's possible to spot meteors – or shooting stars to give them their more romantic title – on any clear night, when, with a bit of luck and not too much light pollution, you can generally see about six an hour.

In August, however, the spectacular Perseids meteor shower passing overhead means you can see as many as 100 an hour. The Perseids are the most famous and most observed of meteors and however short your child's attention span, they are pretty much guaranteed to see something. With the evenings also typically warmer at this time of year, it's the ideal moment for beginners, and anyone interested in seeing their first meteor, to get started.

Meteors are flashes of light caused by particles of cosmic dust burning up as they enter the Earth's atmosphere, about 60 miles above our heads. In the case of the Perseids, these particles were originally part of the Swift-Tuttle comet. The best time to look out for them is just before dawn, when the moon will have set and our side of the Earth will be moving directly into the cloud of debris. The best views will be out in the countryside, but even city folk will be able to wonder at the streaks of light across the sky.

See the National Maritime Museum website: nmm.ac.uk

HELEN DAVIES

Swim in the open air

✳

WHEN it's still warm enough to swim outside, why not leave the steamy, chlorine-soaked, noise-filled air of the indoor pool for the freshness and exhilaration of swimming in a lido?

In their 1930s heyday there were over 400 lidos in this country. After years of neglect three-quarters have gone, but there are still nearly a hundred pools, most of which reopen for the summer. Lidos are often large, with space for sunbathing and a cafe, and have fewer rules than indoor pools. We go armed with an inflatable crocodile, mega swimming-ring and beach ball. Not to mention large towels, a picnic and a book. The lido is really an urban beach.

There has been a recent revival of interest both in outdoor swimming and in the pools' histories. Campaigns have sprung up to protect remaining lidos, and some of them are quite historic. Tooting Bec Lido (south London) celebrated its centenary in 2006, and Hampstead Heath lido celebrated its 70th anniversary in 2008. To find a lido near you go to www.lidos.org.uk

JULIET RIX

Wild Swim by Kate Rew is published by Guardian Books.

Learn woodland survival skills

✳

O NE thing intrigued me in Cormac McCarthy's apocalyptic novel *The Road* – how could the father light a fire without matches? So in the interests of adventure and discovery, we headed off for a junior bushcraft weekend in West Sussex to learn fire-making and other woodland survival skills.

With three other families, we coppiced hazel wood to make a shelter and a pot stand, slung a hammock, whittled with very sharp knives, and learned essential woodland survival tips such as never sleep under a beech tree (because a branch may break off and fall on your head). For fire-making, look out for thistledown and King Alfred's cakes (aka crampball fungus, which grows only on ash trees), both of which make fantastic tinder.

The next day, we tried two fire-making techniques: spark and friction. It is much harder than you imagine: once you've got a spark, you need to nurture the flame, by gently blowing and encouraging it to grow ever stronger. Eventually, though, we had a roaring fire over which we boiled water for tea and fried bacon. Come the apocalypse, we'll be ready.

For details of our course go to www.wildwoodbushcraft.com or search the internet to find a bushcraft course near you. For more ideas go to www.heartandhome.net

TAMSIN WIMHURST

Find tree folk

✳

WHEN our children were younger, we used to enliven a walk in the woods by inventing stories of woodland folk who lived there. Tales of pixies and elves do not have to be elaborate to inspire, especially when a summer breeze is rustling leaves and shafts of sunlight create dancing shadows.

The next step was encouraging the girls to hunt for faces in the bark of old trees, which generated further stories in our flagging repertoire.

The search for tree people can become addictive. Look carefully enough and you really can see faces on some tree trunks; the more you look the more you see. Take along a camera or sketch-pad and get the children to record their finds.

Certain species, especially those with soft bark, provide most potential.

Gnarly old cedars are ideal: we discovered a wizened old man, complete with deep eye sockets, warty nose, long beard and bushy eyebrows, in one. Ancient yews, found in country churchyards, also have potential.

Finding these 'creatures' takes time and patience, though that tends to make for a longer, more satisfying walk for adults. Tree folk are elusive, and there will be shouts of joy when one is discovered. Take a compass and map (woods can become disorienting when searching) – getting lost may give you one story you won't want to recite.

BOB BARTON

Build a treehouse

※

OK, I'll come clean: it's not really a treehouse, and I didn't build it myself. What it resembles most is a dog kennel on stilts jammed up against the fence at the back of our small garden: but it was worth every penny I spent to buy it and then have it put up. My two youngest children – Miranda is seven, Catriona three – sat all day on the lawn watching their new den being assembled, which made it seem a reasonable investment before they had even set foot inside. And since it's been up they've rarely been in the house: one warm day this week I served breakfast, lunch and tea in the treehouse, and there was even a move to go out at 8pm at night for hot chocolate there. Each morning the girls have gathered their props – among others, a pirate ship, a fairy-tale castle, a spy HQ and, with a huge bedroom sheet over the top, an igloo – and headed off to the treehouse for hours. I'm not expecting this to last for ever, it's still got novelty value. But the early indications are good, the potential seems enormous, and the TV has never had such a rest.

JOANNA MOORHEAD

Go fish in the city

✳

LIVING in a big city, nature can seem a long way away. But you can give your children a taste of it by taking them fishing on the canals. First you need to get a licence from the post office or at www.environment-agency.gov.uk/fish. What you want is a 'non-migratory trout, char, freshwater fish (coarse fish) and eels — full season'. Then you need some equipment — a rod, a reel, tackle and a net will suffice. And some bait. If maggots make you squirm, bread or sweetcorn will do. Then you just need a child.

Now the trick with fishing and young, restless children is to bring other distractions. Biscuits and other nibbles are a must. But a bike is also useful. When my seven-year-old gets twitchy after catching nothing for 10 minutes, he goes for a quick spin along the towpath.

But most of the time we just sit there. I tell him stories. He asks me questions I struggle to answer. We eat and drink. Then the float suddenly dips. Something silvery flashes in the water. He reels it in. A small roach. It is released back into the water. It's a ritual that can get you hooked.

RICK WILLIAMS

Roll in the mud

✳

W HEN I was about eight, a friend of my mother's came up from the country to stay with us in London for the weekend. On the Sunday, we went to Richmond Park. I think my mum's friend thought she was going to Biba and she was in a really bad mood, moaning every time she got her London heels wet. It was when her husband said something snappy about minding 'a little bit of mud' that she flipped. She took me by the hand and pulled me over to a huge puddle and sat down and I did too, and then we found another puddle and rolled about in that one and then another and another, each one boggier than the one before, until we were covered in mud from top to toe, even our hair. I expect the others were either laughing or horrified, but I don't remember because the mud itself, the surprise of it and the fact that it was a grown-up letting go, made it the best fun I'd ever had in my life.

I often think it would be a great thing to do with my kids, roll around in the mud when they don't expect it. I don't know why I don't. Dog poo? Maybe this winter would be a good time to try. Yes, maybe this will be the winter that I do.

SABINE DURRANT

Dig your own trench

✳

'**O**I'VE got some real archaeology 'ere for you, children!' A great way of amusing the kids – and fulfilling your *Time Team* fantasies – is to dig an archaeological trench in your back garden. Remember, it's very important you don't call it a hole. A trench or test pit gives that veneer of archaeological respectability. Our house was built in 1870; choosing a piece of garden likely to have been used as a Victorian rubbish tip, I used my fork and shovel to create a two-foot square pit, which we named trench one. The girls were fascinated. A garden trowel and paint scraper helped add an air of professionalism.

What my daughters really loved was getting dirty, sifting soil and washing any finds in a plastic bowl of water. And, amazingly, there was stuff down there. We found fragments of old blue and white china that came up beautifully when washed, rusty bits of metal, an animal bone, pieces of glass, a slate and several worms. Even the odd fragment of flowerpot became Roman treasure to my five-year-old. Then it was time for backfilling and the placing of our finds in a labelled Tupperware container.

Now, whenever we walk past roadworks, the children start looking for finds, and we've even unearthed a Victorian Soyer and Co lemonade bottle in the spoil from a water pipe.

PETE MAY

Mess about by the water

❋

MOST kids are fascinated by boats, what makes them float and not least the idea of them sinking. However, if you are thinking 'boats' don't just automatically head for the coast, as half of us live less than five miles from a canal or river. As a child I often nipped over the M1 motorway bridge to the Grand Union Canal for family walks armed with a pair of heavy binoculars and *Birds of Britain*. I've also spent many a long interlude with my own two children watching locks fill up and empty out, having to explain how and why it's done. I've also found that many of the people who live on boats are more than happy to give you a tour if you have a small and very fascinated child with you. If you aren't lucky enough to get invited in, many canals run their own narrow-boat trips. British Waterways has a website (www.waterscape.com/in-your-area) where you can key in your postcode and find out what's on your doorstep from towpath cycling (for some you'll need a free permit), canoeing, fishing and boat hire to info about waterside picnic sites and family friendly pubs.

JO MEARS

Play days

Games old and new

Learn the basics of chess

※

LEARNING the basics of chess takes about half an hour. Learning to play chess takes a lifetime. The artist Marcel Duchamp gave up painting in the 1920s in order to devote himself to playing chess. 'I am still a victim of chess,' he wrote in 1952. 'It has all the beauty of art – and much more. It cannot be commercialised.'

To begin, you need a board. The best chessboards are homemade. To make a simple one, paint 64 squares of eight rows and eight columns in two contrasting and alternating colours on a piece of wood. You will also need some chess pieces. The best ones are not homemade. Buy some Staunton chess pieces (houseofstaunton.com).

Now you will need a good book. Or access to the internet. Classic chess books include Harry Golombek's *The Game of Chess* (1954) and IA Horowitz and PL Rothenberg's *The Complete Book of Chess* (1969). You might be lucky enough to find one of these in the library, but if you want to buy a book on chess, you'll find the recently updated edition of David Pritchard's *The Right Way to Play Chess* (first published in 1950) a lot easier to get hold of. It explains how to play the game, covers basic theory and includes many examples of play so is ideal for beginners.

IAN SANSOM

The Right Way to Play Chess by David Pritchard is published by Right Way.

Play a game of living chess

✳

CHESS is a difficult game for kids to learn. This is no surprise as there are many pieces, all of which have a special function. The easiest way to teach chess to kids is to make them live the part. You do this by getting them to pretend to be a specific chess piece on a giant board. Any character can be role-played provided they are highly active during the game. I've found that the queen and the knight particularly come to life.

The board can be made from dark-coloured shopping bags for the black squares and sheets of newspaper for the white squares. The other pieces can be drawn on A4 pieces of paper, which the kids can then move. It's important to have a marker to help them remember where they should be standing. Our first game involved the kids taking passive roles, with the game played by adults, but the children were soon moving the pieces themselves.

One of the fun things about living chess is that the kids get to dress up to fit the role. Turn it into a game of speed chess and they also get the equivalent of a medium-level workout at the gym. Children soon grasp the basics and will go on to do very well at the game.

VINCENT REID

Create a board game

✳

I F you are housebound with children, there are worse things you can do than create a board game. All you need are two or three sheets of A4 paper, some scissors, pencils and a bit of imagination.

Board games provide a wealth of learning experiences for children. They can teach abstract maths by providing concrete examples. For example, probabilities: 'You have a one in six chance of landing on the square,' or 'roll a three or more and you win'.

The best benefits for preschoolers are social, where skills can be acquired such as turn taking and learning to deal with winning or losing.

It is best to choose a topic for the game that children know. For younger children, a good idea is an event that is unusual but recognisable, such as visiting the doctor. In our house, Sick Chicken was born on a rainy afternoon. It remains at number one on the request list when we are stuck indoors, even 12 months after its inception.

The aim of Sick Chicken is to visit the doctor and be the first to get home and into bed. A roll of the dice will determine which mode of transport is taken, such as rail, bike or on foot. In order to spice it up, we created random event cards that are drawn on specially coloured squares. These include a flat tyre, a train breakdown or walking through a park as a short cut. On some squares you can skip from one type of transport to another.

Once a player gets to the surgery, they must roll a high

number to be seen by the doctor. This gives other players a chance to catch up. With rules as simple as these, even three-year-olds can fully participate.

And who knows, if children really enjoy your idea, maybe you could sell it to a board game company.

VINCENT REID

Play I Spy

※

EVERYONE loves I Spy With My Little Eye. But nose, ears, fingers and tongue are sadly left out of this game. Anything they can tell you is disregarded if only vision is considered. Next time, try a game of I Hear With My Little Ear. Some kids will find it easier if they close their eyes. The range of sounds that can be heard in the typical house is huge. The gentle hum of the fridge, right through to the drip of drains and the ultrasonic squeal of the stereo on standby are all sounds that we hear every day. So next time you play I Spy, go for a more unusual game that really opens your eyes.

VINCENT REID

Play Pooh Sticks

※

POOH sticks is a great sporting leveller – no matter how much further your opponent can throw or kick a ball, there's no way greater strength or agility can beat you at a game of chance.

Winnie-the-Pooh, in *The House at Pooh Corner*, introduced the world to the wonderfully simple endeavour of dropping a stick from one side of a bridge into a flowing river and waiting to see which player's stick emerges first – and therefore victorious – on the other.

Various strategies for success exist; perhaps the best known is from Ben Schott, miscellany maestro, with his theory of an ideal 'drop zone', suggesting much is in the throw. Or, you could try the deceptively straightforward technique used by a member of the Czech Republic team that won the 2004 World Pooh Sticks Championship, held annually in Little Wittenham, Oxfordshire: he threw his stick in the part of the river he thought was the fastest. But you might prefer to follow the advice of Eeyore who, having won more times than anybody else, said: 'The trick is to drop your stick in a twitchy sort of way.'

ANTONY JONES

Have a game of tiddlywinks

※

My family has just rediscovered tiddlywinks. I'm not sure why sending little coloured discs of plastic plinking into a pot – or not as the case may often be – is quite so amusing, but it is.

Tiddlywinks goes back to Victorian times (patented as Tiddledy Winks in 1888) but the modern game began with some unathletic 1950s Cambridge undergraduates in search of a sport at which they could represent the university. The official game (yes, there are national and international tournaments!) is played on a felt mat 1.8m by 0.9m with a pot in the middle and base lines at each corner. There are four colours (blue, green, red and yellow) and you can play in pairs or singles. The idea is to use a squidger (large plastic disc) to flick winks (small plastic discs) into the pot, or to squop – ie wreck your opponents chances by landing your wink on top of his.

We play obstacle tiddlywinks, where glasses, books, mobile phones or whatever else happens to be on the kitchen table stays put and we have to flick our winks over or round them. We are very good at the scrunge (where the wink bounces out of the pot) but haven't quite worked out the boondock!

The English Tiddlywinks Association: www.etwa.org

JULIET RIX

Play beach cricket

❋

'WHAT do you mean there are no winners in beach cricket?' asked my fiercely competitive nine-year-old nephew.

There are no teams, I explained, one person bats; the rest try to get him or her out. One person bowls for as long as they like, or until someone else wants a go — none of that six balls an over malarkey — while everyone else fields. The batter, meanwhile, tries to hit the ball as far as possible, or maybe attempts a cheeky cover drive into a nearby rock pool, forcing a fielder to get wet when retrieving the ball. For the batter, running is optional, but nobody really keeps any score anyway. You're out when you're caught or the ball hits your wicket – which is whatever is available and can be anything from a cool box to the batsman's own legs. That said, there's no umpire so it's not always clear and often up for shouty discussion. One more thing, a passing dog will steal the ball and run to the other end of the beach with it – that's the closest thing to a rule.

So, nobody wins – it's just fun.

'Hmm,' he replied. 'Can we play two-a-side football instead?'

ANTONY JONES

Play in-the-car games

✳

'ARE we nearly there yet?' Long, boring car journeys aren't much fun for anybody, but some simple, well-targeted games can make the trip fly by. I Spy is a popular fallback, but doesn't work well on motorways or with very young children. We play the car colour game – our unscientific research has found yellow to be the rarest mass-market vehicle colour, so the first passenger to spot one wins top marks. There are fewer points for green and red. Unusual or custom colours such as pink or orange win bonus points, but common ones such as silver, black, blue and white score zero.

Each car can only be scored once, and vans and trucks deserve a game of their own. Agree the duration of each heat and, to avoid squabbles, some diplomatic refereeing is required. You may also have to change the score values to suit personal favourite colours.

Another winner in the Barton jalopy is the Mine a Mint game. Each competitor places a mint sweet (the sort with the hole, preferably sugar-free) on end of their tongue. The person who keeps their sweet intact the longest wins.

No finger contact with the sweet is allowed once in position. It is not as easy as it sounds – concentration and willpower are required. This diversion works with all ages and even the driver can play. As it's not conducive to talking, contemplation is possible. Award a bonus point to the competitor who comes up with the most original thought at the end of a round. Never was silence so sweet.

BOB BARTON

One potato, two potato

※

A LL good seeking and chasing games start with counting out – an efficient, fair way to decide who will be 'it'. When I was a child, if speed was of the essence, we used to do 'Ip, dip, skip, sky blue, who's it, not you.' If we wanted to eke things out a bit we'd do 'potatoes'. To play, everyone would make fists – or potatoes – with both hands (including the nominated counter). Then, huddled in a circle, potato/fists out, the counter would recite 'one potato, two potato, three potato, four,' (with a pause here for effect) 'five potato, six potato, seven potato more,' rapping each 'potato' with his fist on the count of each word. When he got to his own potatoes, he rapped his fists on his chin. If the counter rapped one of your potatoes on the word 'more', the potato was 'out' and had to be put behind your back. If the counter's potatoes were both out, he had to count with his elbows. As the rhyme was repeated, the number of potatoes was whittled down. The last potato was 'it'.

There are lots of variations on counting games that have been passed down the generations. Get them to teach you one that's hot stuff in the playground now, and rack your brains to remember one from your own days. Try this, recorded in *Children's Games in Street and Playground* by Iona and Peter Opie (Oxford Paperbacks):

Red white and blue
The cat's got the flu
The baby has the whooping cough
And out goes you!

JUDITH EAGLE

177

Have a game of conkers

✳

G IVEN the number of conkers found under foot, today's children don't know about this precious, autumnal booty. If you do one thing in the autumn, tell your children about conkers, then perhaps the venerable playground game of the same name – first recorded in 1848 – will live to see another generation.

The fruit of the horse chestnut falls to the ground in September and October, splitting to reveal within its green spiky case, a perfect, polished brown nut. The trees, native to the Balkans, were imported in the 16th century, largely as ornamental trees, which is why you will find conkers gracing urban avenues and parks. The horse chestnut is under serious threat of disease, another reason to go searching for conkers while you can.

When you get them home, soak them in vinegar or bake them in the oven to toughen them up. Bore a hole through the middle (younger children should obviously be supervised). Thread a piece of string, about 25cm long, through the hole. Tie a knot in the end to stop the conker falling off.

Take turns to aim a strike at your opponent's conker (each player wraps the top bit of string around their hand; the person waiting to be bashed lets their string hang straight; the one doing the bashing swings theirs down).

The first conker to break loses. If both are 'virgins', the winner is a one-er. If you beat a one-er, you become a two-er – the world record is held by a 5,000-er.

SARAH WOODLEY

———◆———

Learn to play some old games

✳

Ihave to admit I was a bit taken aback when I discovered that my daughters and their friends had never heard of leapfrog. We were on a picnic at Eltham Palace, south-east London, and the lawns were temptingly manicured, so my friend Ruth and I tucked our skirts into our knickers and showed the young whippersnappers how it was done! After initial screams of embarrassment they were hooked and still leapfrogging around at closing time.

And now if you find yourself harking back to an age of innocence before the lure of Nickelodeon, Nintendo and MySpace, you have no excuse. *The Games We Played*, published by English Heritage (www.english-heritage.org. uk), is an A-Z of games from days gone by. Compiled with the help of members, it features everything from Grandmother's Footsteps and Oranges and Lemons to the rather rough but extremely popular British Bulldog.

NIKKI SPENCER

The Games We Played by Susan Kelleher is published by English Heritage.

Play a game of cards

*

WHEN Buckaroo has lost its charm, half the pieces from Mousetrap are missing and you're wondering if your children are entirely lost to computer games, it's time to turn to Pontoon. It's precisely because Pontoon is 'grown up', and because it involves (dare I say it?) betting, that this simple card game hits pretty much all the buttons for kids. All you need is a pack of cards and a pocketful of pennies. If you object to gambling for money, you could substitute tiddlywinks or matchsticks, but we find there's nothing like the glamour of hard cash to get young brains engaged.

The aim is get the cards in your hand to add up to 21, or as near as you can. You bet on whether or not you'll beat the banker (a role taken by one of the players, and which often transfers to another with amazing speed).

While the rules are straightforward, there's no lack of heady excitement. There's always a flutter when the first two cards you're dealt are an ace and a king, giving you outright Pontoon. Then there's dashing disappointment as you push your luck too far and go bust. And there's that unbearable anticipation when you're asking for the fifth card to make your five-card trick. Pontoon teaches kids some important lessons about risk, luck and judgment. It's about the adrenaline rush of winning, but also it's about learning to lose. Dealing with inevitable let-downs can be hard at first for children, but you're laying some valuable life-skill foundations here.

The game gets very exciting as the stakes rise. Each round only takes a few minutes, and although there's a large dollop of luck involved, skill can play an increasing part as you improve. And don't tell the kids, but they get some maths practice without even realising it!

Get the full rules of Pontoon at www.pagat.com

LESLEY CARR

Play a kind of travel Scrabble

✳

THIS is a portable version of Scrabble that doesn't use the board and without any clever long words, so it's brilliant for livening up dull family holiday moments – we managed a game while waiting for our main course in Pizza Express. All you need are Scrabble (or Snatch) tiles, piled in the middle of a table. Each person takes 15 letters and, as quickly as they can, forms their own set of interlocking words crossword-style as in Scrabble. You are allowed two-lettered words, making it easier for younger kids. The first person to organise all 15 letters into interlocking words shouts 'time'. Then everyone stops and picks up one more letter, and so on until all the letters in the middle are used up. You can break up your words and re-make them to fit the new letters as they come along. The winner is the first to get all their letters into a crossword correctly or, for variety, the person who scores the longest word.

JANE PHILLIMORE

Wild days

Learning more about animals and nature

Save the birds

✳

IN winter, when insects become harder to find, and seeds and berries are often locked away by snow or frost, birds may struggle to find food. Freezing weather is a potential death sentence for many but by feeding the birds in your garden, you can help them survive the worst of the winter. Just a little water, food and shelter can turn your garden into a vital haven.

Follow the RSPB's wild bird winter survival plan to help wildlife during the harshest weather:

1 Put out feed regularly, especially in severe weather. Set up a bird table and use high-calorie seed mixes. This can also be used to put out kitchen scraps such as animal fats, grated cheese and soaked dried fruit.

2 Put out hanging feeders for black sunflower seeds, sunflower hearts, sunflower-rich mixes or unsalted peanuts.

3 Ensure a supply of fresh water every day. If it is very cold use tepid water.

4 Put out fruit, such as apples and pears, for blackbirds, song thrushes and other members of the thrush family.

5 Food bars or fat hung up or rubbed into the bark of trees will help treecreepers, goldcrests and many other species.

6 Put up nest boxes to provide roost sites for the smaller birds. They will then be used for breeding later in the year.

More information about garden wildlife and how to help birds, mammals and insects is available at www.rspb.org.uk/hfw

GEMMA ROGERS

Take a greyhound for a walk

IF your children long for a dog but you are less than keen, how about making friends with a retired greyhound? These graceful, good-natured dogs are in need of pooch-pampering volunteers to exercise them while they are waiting for adoption. The hounds are cared for by the Retired Greyhound Trust, a national charity that finds homes for thousands of retired greyhounds every year. It has 73 branches around the country full of greyhounds in need of a little exercise.

Long hikes are not necessary – after several years chasing a mechanical rabbit for a living, the dogs want nothing more than a couple of gentle 20-minute strolls a day, and staff will fill you in on the dos and don'ts of greyhound-walking.

For details of your nearest kennels visit www.retiredgreyhounds.co.uk

CHRISTINE MORLEY

Tickle a pig

✳

MAYBE it was the AA Milne-style one – knitted for me by my doting gran – that did it. Or reading *Charlotte's Web*. Or my unrequited, childhood love for James Herriot, aka Christopher Timothy (I'm so over him). Whatever the catalyst, for as long as I can recall I've had a thing for pigs and, particularly, piglets.

So imagine my joy, on becoming a mother, to discover we lived within striking distance of not one but three children's farms, where I could indulge my passion while using my son as cover. Fortunately, the 'pig thing' proved genetic.

Far from being gross, pigs are actually grossly maligned and have the cognitive ability to be quite sophisticated. Even more so than dogs and certainly three-year-olds.

But despite their intelligence, we've balked at bringing the chess set. Nope, for us the most fun's to be had with a bit of 'pig whispering'. The challenge is to see if you can pet a piglet into a trance by stroking them in a very rhythmic way. We've got it down to such a fine art we can get them to flop on to their sides in under a minute: the trick is to tickle them under their armpits – they go bonkers for it. Meanwhile, their parents can be lulled into a transcendental state with a good old scratch around the ears.

But it's not just pigs that love massage; goats go a bit dippy too. (Try using your thumbs to massage out from the centre of the forehead and over the eyes.) So far our goat record stands at around 10 minutes of total stillness, which in goat years is, like, forever. And you know what? After all those roast dinners, it feels good to give something back.

Find details of farms near you at www.aboutbritain.com/animalsallregions.htm

ABIGAIL FLANAGAN

Make your own worm farm

※

IF you ask a keen gardener which living thing is our best
friend, they will tell you that it is not dogs, but worms.
Without worms it would be quite difficult to decompose dead
things and turn yesterday's banana skin into tomorrow's
nutrient-rich earth. One way in which we can get to better
know our annelid friends is to make and maintain a worm
farm. It is also a great way of getting rid of kitchen scraps and
turning them into high quality compost.

Worms like darkness and dampness (but not flooded soil).
An old waste-paper basket or planter will do, provided you
have a lid for it. First, drill some holes in the bottom of your
worm farm and in the sides, to allow for water drainage and
oxygen. Then place some satsuma-sized stones in the bottom
for drainage. Cover this layer with scrunched-up damp
newspaper. Then place a layer of compost or high-quality
garden earth on top.

Worms can be bought from garden centres: five hundred
should do. Provided you give them a brief watering every week
and keep them fed, your worms will thrive and multiply.

Your worms will like most fruit and vegetable scraps, though
they are not so keen on citrus fruit. Start off by putting a few
scraps at one side of the farm. You can then monitor the time
it takes for them to eat their food. The only downside to these
pets is that it is very difficult to tell them apart, making it
hard to give them names.

VINCENT REID

189

Take a hawk for a walk

*

Two Harris hawks swoop past our heads and settle on my sons' gloved hands. We are taking the hawks for a walk – or they are taking us. The birds just want the food we hold up for them. We, on the other hand, are enthralled by their every elegant move, and by the very fact that we – with no experience whatsoever – are participating directly in the ancient 'sport of kings'.

Interest in birds of prey is burgeoning and centres around the country are now offering not only bird displays but 'encounters' that involve flying the birds yourself. Our day, on a farm on the edge of London, included feeding a vulture, holding and stroking falcons, ruffling the neck feathers of an eagle (he likes it!) and taking an owl on an outing.

Best of all, though, we felt the magic of a real bird of prey taking off and returning to our very own gloved fists.

Search online for a falcolnry near to you.

JULIET RIX

Tiptoe through snowdrops

O N the face of it, February, when some of us still have our heating on constant, may not seem like the best time to recommend venturing outside for a walk in the woods. But visitors to country estates and gardens around the UK at this time of year are rewarded with a sight that will make putting on all those layers more than worthwhile.

You don't have to be a gardening fanatic to appreciate acre upon acre of pure white snowdrops miraculously springing to life when all around is still virtually dormant. It's a sign that spring is just round the corner.

Each year dozens of English Heritage, National Trust and other historic gardens have special snowdrop openings so the public can appreciate the breathtaking displays. Just remember not to pick the flowers.

For more information on snowdrop openings visit www.nationaltrust.org.uk, www.english-heritage.org.uk and www.eastonwalledgardens.co.uk

NIKKI SPENCER

Become a phenologist

※

'IN the spring a young man's fancy lightly turns to thoughts of love,' to quote Alfred Lord Tennyson, in his poem, *Locksley Hall*. But when does spring begin?

Strictly speaking, spring begins at the vernal equinox, 'vernal' meaning something happening or occurring in the spring (vernal showers, vernal flowers, vernal thoughts of love). The vernal equinox occurs around March 20/21. The sun moves north. So, it's spring. No better time to become a phenologist.

Phenology is the study of the timing of natural events, such as when you see the first swallow, hear the first cuckoo or see the blackthorn blossom. Traditional data on phenology, which goes back to 1736 in the UK, shows that spring is now being sprung 10-30 days earlier. It's vital that this valuable information on seasonal occurrences continues to be collected because it demonstrates how climate change is affecting our wildlife habitats. So look out for frog spawn, bluebells, ladybirds, and blue tits. And go to www.naturescalendar.org.uk to find out more about how you can become a phenologist.

IAN SANSOM

Go on a bluebell walk

DISCOVERING a carpet of bluebells on a woodland walk is one of the great thrills of springtime. This delicate bloom consistently comes top in surveys of the most popular wild flowers. They seem to start flowering earlier each year, but displays are at their most glorious between mid-April and late May, so pack a picnic and go on a bluebell hunt.

Britain has half the world's population of the native bluebell (*Hyacinthoides non-scripta*), yet its existence is threatened, so resist the temptation to pick them. A combination of being dug up and the invasion of two non-native species, the Spanish bluebell and a hybrid, has necessitated their protected status. Yet, year after year, the clever bulbs manage to sprout, bud and bloom before the tree canopy has time to block the precious sunlight.

The Ramblers' Association has a programme of over 100 guided bluebell walks, which run between April and June each year. Held all over the country, they are free to everyone and no booking is required. Details are on its website, www. ramblers.org.uk. The National Trust also has bluebell walks at many of its parks and gardens, including the Ashridge estate, Berkhamsted in Hertfordshire and Hatchlands Park, Surrey.

Though mainly woodland flowers, don't be surprised to also see them elsewhere, like Snowdonia. Bluebells form part of country folklore: legend says the woodland fairies are summoned by their ringing. So do tread carefully and listen out for any unusual sounds in the breeze.

BOB BARTON

Play spot the species

✳

WOODLAND is usually full of trees, shrubs and wild flowers. The problem is that most flora look very similar, leading some children to wistfully think about their computer games when walking in the woods. One way to engage kids with the outdoors is to make them botanists. This can be achieved without sending them off to do a BSc. All you need to do is find a wood and the Wildlife Trust (www.wildlifetrusts.org) will set you off in the right direction. Once there, you can set each child the task of identifying a different genus or species.

One could be charged with spotting fungi, another parasitic plants and a third conifers. Whoever sees the most at the end of the walk is the winner, with consolation prizes for second and third place. Another game is to identify plants from their leaves, with points scored for each leaf that is correctly identified. This can also be turned on its head, with unidentified leaves scoring points. If your kids really love the outdoors, they can always join the Wildlife Trust youth branch at www.wildlifewatch.org.uk and do all sorts of wholesome things like counting frogs, looking at badgers and saving otters.

VINCENT REID

Listen out for the birds

WE always plan to listen to the May dawn chorus, but it's unbearably early – even for early rising children and insomniacs. So I decide to impress my daughters with the best birdsong performances of the evening. If you can finish work early before the middle of June (and live in the south of England) why not head for the sort of thicket where you can hear a song thrush repeating every note three times, a tiny wren do opera, or the machine-gun melodies favoured by the courting nightingale?

At Lee Valley, a short walk from Cheshunt train station, Lola, nine, Nell, seven, and my twitcher friend, Roger, are constantly distracted by melodies on our way to hear the nightingales. There's the whinny of the little grebe frolicking on the lake; the summer boom of the cuckoo; the wood pigeon asking 'Why are my toes bleeding, Betty?' and the great tit's shout for 'Teacher! Teacher!' With all this noise, we nearly miss the enigmatic Hungarian visitor – a red-footed falcon hawking for dragonflies. Nearby, 20 swifts are picking off smaller insects. 'That can't be a hobby,' says Roger excitedly. He grabs his binoculars and tells us to look for a pale head, pinkish belly and a barred tail. Despite this excellent description of a goblin, both girls locate the bird and watch a show of diving and 180 degree turns at high speed (www.rspb.org.uk)

NICOLA BAIRD

Hug a tree (to find how old it is)

✳

THE Woodland Trust wants your kids to be tree-huggers. It's all part of the Ancient Tree Hunt – hugging a tree is a respectable scientific way of measuring a tree's age. If a tree's trunk is so big it requires three or more friends to link arms around it, then the trust wants to know about it.

Anything that looks big enough to come alive on *Doctor Who* will be added to the Woodland Trust's living database. Tree trackers are also invited to upload photos and stories about their favourite trees on to a specially designed website.

Although the Woodland Trust knows where some of Britain's ancient trees are, few are recorded in detail. It's particularly interested in huge trees in urban areas. 'We're asking people to look out for trees that are particularly old, fat or gnarled,' says the president of the Woodland Trust, Clive Anderson.

Your child might spot a previously unrecorded 1,000-year-old oak or a tree that started its life under Henry VIII and which now has his girth. Top trees might even become Tree of the Moment (and appear on the Woodland Trust's website). Hopefully, the children might find a rival to the Major Oak in Sherwood Forest, a 'druid's tree' with a 7.3m girth called the Muggington Yew or the 1,000-year-old Bowthorpe Oak in Lincolnshire, a tree that once fitted 39 people inside it.

Let fat, old trees get under your skin by hugging and recording their details at www.ancienttreehunt.org.uk. Or call the Woodland Trust on 08452 935650.

PETE MAY

Go on a badger watch

＊

IF their recent (mostly negative) press is to be believed, Britain is teeming with badgers. But try to actually see one and you might think differently. As a family, we have been attempting to see badgers for years.

Controversy aside, they are remarkable, little understood mammals and most children love them. So this summer we decided to get serious.

We wound our way down country lanes to Devon Badger Watch (five miles north of Tiverton), home to farmers-turned-badger-experts Kevin and Anne and 'the Barton Clan' of six wild badgers, whose territory spreads over 24 hectares.

We sit silently in a wooden hide listening to Kevin tell us in a quiet monotone all about badgers – their powerful teeth, extreme timidity and odd living arrangements. Suddenly, there he is: a perfect stripey head and grey, furry body, big digging claws, tiny eyes and little folded-back ears – a real badger just 50cm away. This, we are told, is Hopalong (so called because he recently hurt his leg). He is soon joined by three more badgers and then a fourth. We hold our breath and watch. They are so close we can hear them munching, look into their faces, see every hair on their backs.

They stay for maybe 15 minutes jostling and eating before scampering off into the woods. When we are far enough from the hide to talk again, the boys give a simple verdict: 'Wow!'

April to October. Phone 01398 351506 or go to www.devonbadgerwatch.co.uk

JULIET RIX

Breed butterflies

✳

THE caterpillars arrived in a small brown box delivered by the postman. Inside was a plastic pot with air holes in the lid, green gungy food in the bottom and five tiny caterpillars. They set about growing at an extraordinary rate – just like the Very Hungry Caterpillar.

They doubled in size in a week and after a fortnight began to wrap themselves in silky thread. Two gave up at this point, but the other three became J-shaped chrysalids hanging from the lid. We transferred them to the butterfly habitat – a large pop-up gauze cylinder – and watched and waited.

In due course the chrysalids went dark and you could just see colours through the casing. The next time we looked there was a butterfly stretching out its wings. The undersides were brown but when the wings opened we knew why they were called painted ladies. Two more butterflies followed until we were able to release Robert, Oscar and Charles into their real habitat – the great wide world.

Robert did a lap of honour around our heads, while the other two flew straight off to some flowering trees nearby. We hope they're still out there, laying eggs (despite their names) that will turn into more caterpillars.

Butterfly Garden kit, Insect Lore, www.insectlore.co.uk, 01726 860273. Caterpillars are sent out from March to mid-September only.

JULIET RIX

Study moths

※

Do moths really have a death wish, or is this just a moth myth? National moth night takes place once a year in the UK and is as good a time as any to find out. Across the country, an army of moth-watching volunteers collect data about moths, including many threatened species. You can join in at one of many public events, or try DIY lepidoptery at home.

First, attract your moths. Get the children to help brew up a special sticky potion with black treacle and cola, which they paint on to tree trunks, then train a strong light outside on to a white sheet. Then it's a matter of waiting until it gets dark before you check who's come to dinner.

In Britain, there are more than 900 species of moths. The best time to study them is between spring and early autumn. In the winter you can look for chrysalises and you often also disturb Peacocks or Small Tortoiseshells hibernating in curtains, sheds etc. But most of the observation work takes place between April to September leaving the winter months free to write up your data!

National moth night takes place on a different date each year to focus on different parts of the season (to find out when this is, check www.nationalmothnight.info). If you record your data properly, your results will go towards building a detailed survey of moths across Britain. The website also has tons of information including identification guides, recipes for attracting moths, an online reporting form and details of the public events around the country. A great excuse for a late night!

LESLEY CARR

Take a whale-watching trip

※

You could be forgiven for thinking a whale-watching trip would cost far more than your bank account can take, given that you apparently need to travel to the Azores, Iceland or even Singapore for the best sightings. But you will find 26 species of cetacean (whales, dolphins and porpoise) in UK waters – including killer whales.

Mid August to the end of September is the best time to catch them. Certain coastal points are prime (Scotland, west Wales, Devon and Cornwall), but wherever you live you will find marine visitors not too far away – even in the shallow south coastal waters you can see porpoise and bottlenose dolphins.

'A lot depends on the weather – if it's good then you have a good chance of seeing various types of species,' says Dr Peter Evans, director of the Sea Watch Foundation. Its website has excellent advice on the best locations, including beaches and bays where you won't even need to leave dry land to see some whale action. Go to www.seawatchfoundation.org.uk

ANTONY JONES

Be a wildlife detective

＊

FANCY finding out more about the area you live in and the wildlife that shares it with you? The Royal Society for the Protection of Birds' WildSquare project not only ticks all the boxes but it will also get the kids ticking them too.

The idea is to 'adopt' a 1km squared area nearby that you can survey for all sorts of wildlife over the coming months. First off, go to www.rspb.org.uk/wildsquare, register your details and choose your WildSquare. It can be wherever you want – but it makes sense for it to be somewhere you visit regularly, like a local park or nature reserve. In return you'll receive an exclusive WildSquare folder, calendar and sticker pack with information on what to do next.

From one season to the next, you'll be told what to look out for and there are detailed identification and survey sheets to print out to help you. Your findings will help the RSPB build up a valuable picture of the natural world we live in but rarely slow down long enough to notice.

ABIGAIL FLANAGAN

Go on a fungal foray

✳

IT'S amazing how much fun a family walk can be when you're on the trail of weirdly shaped and wonderfully coloured fungi such as witches' butter, penny buns and jelly ears.

Despite their whimsical names, fungi are a crucial part of the natural world. They quietly recycle dead wood, leaves and animals, and provide nutrition for plants. They keep us in bread, beer, blue cheese and penicillin, not to mention swanky delicatessens. Amateur fungi detectives can have lots of fun identifying different types when they appear in the autumn. You can either take them on a fungal foray led by an expert, such as those run by the Forestry Commission (www.forestry. gov.uk), or you can organise one with friends.

If you opt for the latter, head for an area with woodland, preferably beech and oak, or pine, as well as pasture, which is good for field mushrooms. Take a guidebook to help with identification, such as *Mushrooms and Toadstools of Britain* by Brian Spooner or *Mushrooms* by Roger Phillips. Take a camera and notebook to record details such as habitat, the shape, colour and texture of the cap, underside, and stem (stipe). Back home you can analyse the flesh, sketch them or make spore prints. To do this, remove the stem and lay the cap on a piece of paper with a bowl covering it. Leave it for two hours by which time the spores will have formed a pattern. Never eat wild fungi unless it has been identified by an expert, and wash your hands after handling them.

SHARON SWEENEY-LYNCH

Special days

Ideas for the holidays

Create a bird's nest at Easter

✳

MUFFLE up and make birds' nests with your children. First, frogmarch them out to collect nest-building materials such as clay, mud, moss, lichen, twigs, feathers, stems, sheep's wool or spiders' webs. Weave the twigs and stems together to make the base of the nest then line it with mud and soft things. Shape and size do not matter, but it must hold together. For more of a challenge, get a bird book from the library that has photos of nests and try making one for a particular species.

Smaller children like putting these nests into hedges or shrubs to see if the birds will use them (they won't). But you can also turn the nests into Easter decorations: hard-boil or blow some eggs, then decorate them. You can soak them in vinegar and food-colouring overnight (if you draw on them with wax crayons first, you get lovely patterns), or paint them with nail varnish or glitter glue, or make them into faces with marker pens and wobbly stick-on eyes. Then put them in the nest.

Alternatively, use homemade nests for an Easter egg hunt: distribute the nests around a garden, park or wood and get the 'Easter Bunny' to fill them with small chocolate eggs. Then let loose a horde of chocoholic children.

LUCY ATKINS

Go on an Easter egg hunt

✳

O R, make them work a bit harder for their chocolate. First, blow some eggs: pierce a hole in each end of a hen's egg, then blow the contents out into a bowl (omelettes all round!) Poke a written clue, rolled up, inside each egg. Each clue should lead to the next, so you might want to number each egg as you insert the clue so you don't forget the order. The final clue should lead to a stash of eggs (perhaps in a homemade nest).

Hide the clue-containing eggs around your home or garden, and let the desperate children decipher their way to the chocolate egg stash, smashing eggs as they go to get to the clues.

If you have kids of different ages, it might be an idea to do separate hunts with different age-appropriate clues (even small children can work out pictorial clues, or simple written clues that are read to them).

If this all sounds like hard work, you can always get someone else to do the whole thing for you: the National Trust runs chocolate Easter egg hunts in nearly 200 venues around the country (www.nationaltrust.org.uk).

LUCY ATKINS

Make an Easter piñata

※

FROM Mexico, south (and now also in the Latinised US) America, you buy a piñata for every family event, as both party game and goodie-bags. It's a very breakable container of thin, unbaked clay or papier-mâché: these bases are glammed-up with layers of fringed, shredded tissue or crepe paper. Traditional shapes are a globe, star, or lamb, but market vendors also sell approximations of movie cartoon characters.

The idea is to leave a hole in the shell through which to insert a payload of sweets plus small toys; then to hang it from a beam, doorway or branch; then children, sometimes blindfolded, take turns to hit it with a stick until it shatters and everybody scrambles for the contents. A less violent variant, easier to manage at home, has an exit hole plugged with tightly balled-up paper to which is attached a tail of bright twine and/or streamers. Many such tails dangle from all over the piñata: everybody has a chance to tug, but only one will pull the plug and release the goodies. If you have space for mess, it's possible to work up a classic piñata from modelling clay rolled out into thin, flat sheets, then moulded over a blown-up large balloon.

More realistically, tape all the flaps shut on a decent-sized cardboard box, punch two small holes in the top for a string from which to suspend it; make two more holes, one in the top and another in the base, big enough for filling and emptying. Push the paper plug deep into the exit hole making sure its tail is firmly attached. Fringe strips of paper and glue them all over the box: this is the fun part. Glue many fake tails around the bottom of the box. For Easter, fill with creme eggs, bags of mini-eggs, toy chicks, etc.

VERONICA HORWELL

Make a portrait of mum for Mother's Day

✳

Dads, don't be total spanners – plan ahead and save yourselves untold grief. Yes, we're talking Mother's Day. And no, we don't want a bunch of battered carnations from the garage – ever again. Instead, we'd like something the kids (and you) have put a little thought into. (Even if we've had to put that little thought into you.) Something heartfelt and homemade that we'll cherish for eternity. Essentially, get the kids painting.

Narcissists we may be, but nothing will melt our hearts more than a picture of 'My mum'. Portrait artist (and mum) Diane McLellan has these tips for assisting your budding Rembrandts:

'Get kids to focus on the shapes of a head. Heads and eyes aren't round, but oval or almond-shaped respectively. Ears don't normally stick out at right angles, nor can you usually see right up a person's nose. Don't forget the neck, and try to get the proportions right.

'Include distinguishing features, like beauty spots, fringes or partings. Try to also include a signature feature, like a favourite piece of clothing or hobby – it may help with identification!

'Draw in pencil first to get it right, then colour in. For the less dextrous, very young, or those wanting something different, try collage using photographs or prints.

'Finally, remember that end results will look 100 times better if framed or mounted. Try personalising frames by sticking on craft jewels, dried flowers, shells or anything that reflects mum's interests.'

Visit www.dianemclellan.com.

ABIGAIL FLANAGAN

Go trick or treating en masse
at Halloween

✳

BEFORE I had kids, Halloween was about getting home from work and waiting for that first knock on the door with the sinking realisation that there were no 'treats' to be handed out, then hiding for the rest of a miserable evening.

But now it's different. My children (three and five) are well aware of the delightful dressing-up-and-eating-sweeties opportunity presented by the Halloween experience. So far, so slightly daunting. But last year, a neighbour had a brainwave. There are lots of under-fives in our road, so why not get together for a warming drink at around six, then set forth in force – a posse of witches, spooks and black cats – to terrify the street in one swoop. To make it more user-friendly, she posted leaflets a couple of days before, saying: 'Please put a pumpkin or a notice in your window if you wish to be visited. If not, we'll leave you alone.'

And so, on Halloween night, off we went, a giggling, excitable gaggle scampering down the road. Several neighbours rose magnificently to the occasion. One actor manqué howled eerily through his letterbox, then just when the children were becoming seriously worried, flung open the door and challenged them to plunge their hands into a large bowl of 'vomit' to retrieve their treats.

JANE RICHARDS

Make starchy ghosts for Halloween

HANG these ghoulish apparitions around the house or in a window or tree outside to attract trick or treaters. They look even spookier when uplit with a lamp or torch.

You'll need:
An old plastic 1 litre bottle
A tennis (or similar-size) ball
A plastic, child's size, coat hanger
A box of household starch
An old white sheet or muslin, cut into squares
  (ours were 60cm x 60cm butmake them as big
  as you like)
A thick black felt-tip pen

To make the outline of the head, half-fill the plastic bottle with water to stabilise it and, with the lid off, balance the tennis ball on top. For the shoulders, stick the coat hanger on the neck of the bottle with Blu-Tack.

This is your frame. (For more than one starchy ghost, make more frames or re-use this one after each ghost has dried.)

Take two tablespoons of starch, mix in four tablespoons of cold water, then pour a pint of boiling water over the mixture (this is twice as strong as the manufacturer's instructions). Mix thoroughly while the solution is dissolving. Leave to cool for a short while until hand hot.

Then dip a square of white material into the starch mixture. Soak and squeeze it out, then drape over the tennis-ball skeleton. If you want the ghost to stand on a table, arrange its lower edge against a flat surface so it forms a base. Leave for a few hours to dry.

Before taking the ghost off the frame, draw its eyes and a mouth with felt-tip pen. To hang, thread a needle with black cotton, tie a big knot in one end, push the needle through the top of the head from the inside, and make a hanging loop at the top.

JANE PHILLIMORE AND TAMSIN WIMHURST

Play Halloween pop

✳

THIS is a good noisy game to kick off a Halloween party. Blow up three balloons for each person, and tie a piece of thin wrapping ribbon round each one. Each child ties a ribbon and balloon to one of their ankles: the idea is to run around with bare feet (or shoes if you are outdoors) trying to stamp on and pop everyone else's balloons while trying not to get your own stamped on and popped.

Everyone has three lives: when their first balloon is popped, they tie another on their ankle and start again. (Parents might need to cut off the old balloons with scissors.) Everyone counts the numbers of balloons they pop: the winner is the person who has popped most and been popped least.

JANE PHILLIMORE AND TAMSIN WIMHURST

Go apple bobbing and sweet dunking at Halloween

A double whammy of sticky messiness: children get their faces wet apple bobbing, then turn into white-faced banshees when they dip into a pile of flour to dig out their sweet treat.

Lay a plastic mat or black bin liner on the floor. Three-quarters fill a wide, not-too-deep basin (buckets make it difficult for small children) with water, and put on the mat. Float some apples in the water, first taking out the stems, which are too easy to catch.

Take a large plate and a large mixing bowl. Fill the bowl with flour and mix in some sweets (we used plain boiled sweets, though if your kids object to the floury taste, use wrapped ones instead). Put the plate over the basin, turn upside down and place the plate of flour beside the apple-bobbing basin.

Ask the children to dunk in turn: first they bob for apples, and when their faces are dripping wet, they dunk in the flour to find their sweets.

JANE PHILLIMORE AND TAMSIN WIMHURST

Weave a spider's web for Halloween

THESE are made of plastic glue, squirted out of a cold glue gun, and they take about two minutes to create. Drape them around the house with cleverly placed plastic spiders, or use to jazz up the children's trick or treat costumes. Tiny webs can be used as earrings – just add a loop at the top.

You'll need:
A cold glue gun and glue sticks (from any craft store, about £7.00)
Greaseproof paper
Plastic spiders to dot around

Lay the greaseproof paper on a flat surface and, using the glue gun, draw three long lines of glue at 60 degrees to each other, crossing in the centre to make the six spokes of the web. Then fill in the web: starting in the middle, draw crescent-shaped lines between the spokes in rounds.

Continue until the web is full. Leave for a few minutes until dry. Then gently lift the web off the paper – it's ready to use.

JANE PHILLIMORE AND TAMSIN WIMHURST

Build a bonfire on bonfire night

✳

IF you're planning to have a bonfire, try not to build it until the day you plan to set light to it. Not only does this mean your pyre won't have been hostage to the fortune of the weather, but it also limits the likelihood of hedgehogs, who start hibernating around early November, using it to nest in.

Big organised displays may be spectacular but nothing quite beats having family and friends round. First, safety: build your bonfire well away from buildings, sheds, hedges and fences and beware of overhead cables; although there are no specific by-laws to prohibit bonfires, all displays must now be over by midnight (and it's now illegal to set off fireworks after 11pm); use a domestic firelighter rather than anything flammable, and don't light the bonfire if it's very windy. If you're having a firework display, light the bonfire afterwards to avoid accidentally setting off the fireworks.

So what to put on the bonfire? Any dry autumn prunings, crates from the tip or a shop (good for ventilation) and, of course, wood-wise – ash and maple are good; pine spits. Check too that no one has put anything dangerous on the fire such as aerosol cans, paint tins, foam furniture or batteries.

Which just leaves time to start baking the spuds in the oven before transferring to the fire in foil and, later, toasted marshmallows, three or four at a time on a twig over the embers.

CHRIS HALL

Build your own Christmas grotto

IF you prefer the restrained approach when it comes to Christmas decorations, don't expect your kids to thank you. This year, indulge them and the god of all that glitters by helping them to make a bedroom grotto.

Abandon good taste and let rip with the glitz!

You'll need some fairy lights, lots of tinsel and as many of those fiddly, intricate, hanging foil things as you can lay your hands on.

Several evenings were spent cutting and sticking together old-fashioned paper-chains. Instead of lengths of dollies, we made snowmen and Christmas trees, and there was a brave and partially successful attempt at reindeer.

During the hyped-up approach to Christmas, it was surprisingly easy to get the kids upstairs and into bed. And one of the highlights of last December was finding grandad asleep in the fairy grotto, surrounded by twinkly lights, after a little too much festive cheer.

LESLEY CARR

Make mulled wine for kids at Christmas

✳

REASONS why Christmas is ace number 642: mulled wine. On cold December days the aromatic, age-old favourite is simply the perfect drink: warming, spicy and, of course, alcoholic. That is unless you're on driving duty or underage in which case you might have to do with a resolutely non-festive and somewhat feeble hot chocolate alternative.

Given the generous spirit of the season, why not take time to brew a non-alcoholic mulled wine for children and drivers? It's pretty easy – just gather a carton of cranberry juice, the rind of two oranges, about a dozen cloves, four tablespoons of clear honey, a teaspoon of vanilla extract, a couple of cinnamon sticks and some freshly ground nutmeg. Grab a heavy-based saucepan and heat the cranberry juice on the hob. Add the honey and vanilla extract and stir slowly for a couple of minutes. Then drop in the rind, cloves, cinnamon sticks, nutmeg and warm through. That's pretty much it – it's simple, delicious and you can serve with a hangover-free guarantee.

ANTONY JONES

Hide the Christmas presents

✳

HIDING a small selection of the presents on Christmas Day (hiding all of them is simply too sadistic) may deviate from the traditional Father Christmas practice of putting presents in stockings, but it certainly makes the anticipation last a little longer. Create an air of mystery by writing cryptic clues for the whereabouts of the presents in invisible ink. This is fairly easy to make. You just need some onions (not red) or lemons, and then squeeze them to extract their juice and use this as your ink. With a quill pen or a sharpened stick, you write a message on white paper. It can be 'revealed' by simply heating it with an iron.

To avoid too much frustration it is a good idea to put the clues in envelopes (a different colour for each child) because they can be hard to find otherwise! I find that a good way to give even the littlest ones a chance at finding the clues is to connect all of them together by threading them on to a long piece of string that you partially hide.

MELISSA VIGUIER

Days for the diary

Family-friendly events around the country

London International Mime Festival

WHEN: Mid January
WHERE: London Southbank Centre, Barbican Centre and other City venues
COST: Varies by event, some are free
www.mimefest.co.uk

Show-stopping circus arts, puppetry, physical theatre, live art and workshops for all ages.

Russian Winter Festival

WHEN: Mid January
WHERE: Trafalgar Square, London
COST: Free
www.london.gov.uk/mayor/Russian_festival/index.jsp

Celebrating the Russian New Year, the festival offers a taste of Russia to children and adults with traditional music, puppetry and entertainment.

Chinese New Year Celebrations

WHEN: Late January – early February
WHERE: In and around London's Chinatown. Celebrations are also held in larger towns and cities across the UK
COST: Free
www.chinatownchinese.co.uk

Traditional and contemporary Chinese dance and entertainment, delicious Chinese food, fireworks and firecrackers, lion and dragon dances.

World Wetlands Day

WHEN: Early February
WHERE: Events held at all nine Wildfowl and Wetlands Trust centres across the UK
COST: Free to WWT members, otherwise standard entry fees apply
www.wwt.org.uk

Celebrating the importance of Wetland conservation, lots of family fun activities including wetland games and competitions.

Jorvik Viking Festival

WHEN: Mid February
WHERE: Venues in York (Viking *Jorvik*)
COST: Free
www.jorvik-viking-centre.co.uk

Come and meet the Vikings as they descend upon the city for saga telling, arts and crafts, battle re-enactments, drills and demonstrations for all ages.

International Darwin Day

WHEN: Mid February
WHERE: Shrewsbury – Darwin's birthplace – is a focal point for celebrations but events are held throughout the UK and worldwide
COST: Various, some free events. Entry to Darwin's house is £8.80 for adults and £4.40 for children. Concessions apply
www.darwinshrewsbury.org,www.darwinday.org,www.english-heritage.org.uk

Lots of science-themed family fun. Explore Darwin's house and study.

World Book Day

WHEN: Early March
WHERE: Events held in many primary and secondary schools
COST: Free. A £1 book token is given to each child, redeemable against one of six £1 festival books
www.worldbookday.com

The UK and Ireland's celebration of World Book Day, books and reading.

London Frog Day

WHEN: Mid March
WHERE: Various parks/wildlife centres in and around London
COST: Free
www.wildlondon.org

Lots of fantastic froggy fun for all ages – frog-spotting, crafts and educational activities.

National Science and Engineering Week

WHEN: Mid March
WHERE: Various venues throughout the UK
COST: Events are variously priced, some free
www.britishscienceassociation.org/web/nsew

Potions, workshops, demonstrations, puzzles, competitions and activities. Lots of science fun.

Grand National Sheepstake

WHEN: Early April
WHERE: The Big Sheep, Abbotsham, Bideford, North Devon
COST: £9.95 per person. Free for children under three
www.thebigsheep.co.uk

Features the world famous annual Sheep Grand National plus lots of other animal fun including sheep shearing, sheepdog trials and horse whispering.

The London Harness Horse Parade

WHEN: Easter Monday
WHERE: South of England Centre, Ardingly, West Sussex
COST: Adults £5, children free
www.lhhp.co.uk

A chance for enthusiasts to show off immaculately turned out horses. Don't miss Fuller's Brewery shires and the Harrod's Friesians.

International Edinburgh Science Festival

WHEN: Early April
WHERE: Venues across Edinburgh
COST: Varies by event
www.sciencefestival.co.uk

Lots of family-friendly events throughout the city to entertain, mystify and enlighten young minds.

Royal Shakespeare Company's Annual Open Day

WHEN: Late April
WHERE: Stratford-Upon-Avon
COST: Free entry
www.rsc.org.uk

Join the actors for a picnic, learn how they make the blood, guts and gore that appear on stage, and take part in workshops in dance, music, costume and mask making.

St George's Day festivities

WHEN: Late April
WHERE: Locations across England
COST: Varies by event, many are free For comprehensive listings of nationwide events see www.stgeorgesdayevents.org.uk

Traditional English fun, food, re-enactments, medieval clothing, hog roasts, games and activities.

Beltane Fire Festival

WHEN: April 30 (Mayday eve)
WHERE: Carlton Hill, Edinburgh
COST: Free
www.beltane.org

Once a pagan celebration of fertility and the coming of spring, now a good opportunity for a burn up! Fire-jumping and spectacular folk displays.

Downton Cuckoo Fair

WHEN: First May bank holiday weekend
WHERE: Downton, Wiltshire (near Salisbury)
COST: Free entry to town centre events
www.cuckoofair.co.uk

Maypole dancing, bingo, cream teas, clay pigeon shooting, kids entertainment and traditional village fete fun.

International Dawn Chorus Day

WHEN: Early May
WHERE: Organised morning walks take place across the UK
COST: Some events are free
www.idcd.info,www.nationaltrust.org.uk,www.rspb.org.uk,www.wildlifetrust.org.uk

Early risers shouldn't miss this chance to witness nature's very own daily miracle, followed by a hearty breakfast and hot drinks.

Baishaki Mela (Bangla New Year)

WHEN: Mid May
WHERE: Brick Lane, East London
COST: Free
www.visitbricklane.com/baishakimela

Musicians, dancers, traditional dress, delicious curries and a mini food festival, poetry, art, exhibitions and rickshaw rides.

Imaginate Festival

WHEN: Mid May
WHERE: Edinburgh and various venues in Scotland
COST: Varies by event, some are free
www.imaginate.org.uk

The UK's largest performing arts festival for children and young people includes performances, productions and workshops.

Tetbury Woolsack Race

WHEN: Late May
WHERE: Tetbury, Gloucestershire
COST: Free to spectate, race entry is £5 per person
www.tetburywoolsack.co.uk

Competitors run (carrying a 60lb wool sack) through the streets of Tetbury – mostly uphill. An all-day spectacular with all the traditional fun of the fair.

Fierce Festival

WHEN: Mid May – early June
WHERE: Venues throughout Birmingham
COST: Varies by event, some are free
www.myfiercefestival.co.uk

Not all the acts at the UK's 'most eclectic live arts festival' are suitable for kids but don't miss the Fierce Kids Film Project showcasing films shot and directed by children.

Hay Fever at the Hay Festival

WHEN: Late May
WHERE: Hay-on-Wye, Powys, Wales
COST: Varies by event, some are free
www.hayfestival.com

The children's book festival that runs alongside the main event is a chance to meet well-known children's authors as well as take part in drama, dance, storytelling and outdoor events.

Bristol Vegan Fayre
WHEN: Late May/early June
WHERE: Bristol Harbourside
COST: £5 entry fee
www.bristolveganfayre.co.uk

More than 160 stalls, talks and demonstrations plus live music, kids' entertainment and lots of vegan delights to sample.

Cheltenham Science Festival
WHEN: Early June
WHERE: Venues in Cheltenham
COST: Varies by event
www.cheltenhamfestivals.com

Family events and activities including demonstrations, talks and workshops – science will never be boring again.

Community Rail Weekend
WHEN: Early June
WHERE: Stations and rail routes throughout the UK
COST: Varies by event
www.acorp.uk.com/diary.html

Lots of railway fun including rides on non-commercial lines, talks and waving at trains.

Open Farm Sunday
WHEN: Early June
WHERE: Farms and farm parks throughout the UK
COST: Varies by event, some are free
www.farmsunday.org

Find out more about how the food you eat is grown and produced, enjoy farm walks, pond dipping, tractor rides, nature trails, mini-farmers' markets and picnics.

Exhibition Road Fete de la Musique
WHEN: Mid June
WHERE: Exhibition Road, London
COST: Free
www.exhibitionroad.com

Free musical performance and workshops featuring a huge range of styles and sounds – something for all the family.

Bike Week
WHEN: Mid/late June
WHERE: Venues throughout the UK
COST: Events are variously priced
www.bikeweek.org.uk

Get your kids to take on the great de-stabiliser challenge, take a bike skills workshop or watch some top-class bike racing.

Glastonbury Festival Kidz Field
WHEN: Late June
WHERE: Glastonbury, Somerset
COST: All children under 12 admitted free
www.kidzfield.com

Over three acres of fun for children that includes a circus, songs, puppetry, face-painting and a whole host of workshops.

Biggin Hill Air Show
WHEN: Late June
WHERE: Biggin Hill Airport, Kent
COST: £21 for adults, £7 for children. Advance fares and concessions apply. Free for under fives
www.bigginhillairfair.co.uk

Aerial acrobatics, classic and contemporary aircraft and lots of family fun.

Winchester Hat Fair

WHEN: First weekend in July
WHERE: Winchester city centre
COST: Free
www.hatfair.co.uk

The UK's longest-running street theatre festival is named after the tradition of throwing money into performers' hats. Performances, small-scale shows and a programme of community arts and education.

Guardian Family Friendly Museum Award

WHEN: Early July
WHERE: Events take place in short-listed museums, chosen for child-friendly and innovative approaches to learning
COST: Varies by event, some are free
www.guardian.co.uk/kidsinmuseums,
www.kidsinmuseums.org.uk

Short-listed museums provide educational fun for all the family.

Tewkesbury Medieval Festival

WHEN: Early July
WHERE: Fields off Lincoln Green Lane, Tewkesbury
COST: Free
www.tewkesburymedievalfestival.org

Stand back and watch the huge battle re-enactment, then find out more about how medieval people lived, what they ate and try your hand at some medieval crafts too.

Manchester International Festival (biennial festival)

WHEN: Mid July
WHERE: Venues across Manchester
COST: Varies by event, many (particularly those for children) are free
www.mif.co.uk

Showcases pioneering international artists. Don't miss The Great Outdoors – a programme of events and activities for children aged 3 to 11 that takes place in Manchester Town Hall.

The July Project

WHEN: Early-mid July
WHERE: Calderdale
COST: Varies by event, many are free
www.thejulyproject.co.uk

Over 100 fun events and activities for young people aged 6-19: music, photography and cartoon workshops, drama, dance and a chance to try out many new skills.

London Literature Festival

WHEN: Early July
WHERE: London South Bank Centre
COST: Varies by event, some are free
www.southbankcentre.co.uk/literaturefestival

Lots of opportunities to meet children's authors, plus workshops, dramatics, and talks for younger readers.

Summer in the Park (biennial event)

WHEN: Mid July
WHERE: Platt Fields Park, Manchester
COST: Adults £9.50, concessions £6, free for children under 10
www.summerinthepark.co.uk

Food, drink and music with play area, games, workshops and make and bake activities for kids.

World Snail Racing Championships

WHEN: Mid July
WHERE: Congham, Norfolk
COST: Free or nominal entry fee
www.snailracing.net

Part of St Andrew's church fete, pit your snail's talent against 200 other highly trained hopefuls.

Doggett's Coat and Badge Race

WHEN: Mid July
WHERE: River Thames – London Bridge to Chelsea
COST: Free to spectators
www.watermenshall.org/dogget-race

See watermen (and these days, women) in 18th century dress compete for the prize of a scarlet coat, silver arm badge and breeches. The race started in 1715 and is believed to be the oldest sporting contest in continued existence.

Pontefract Liquorice Festival

WHEN: Mid July
WHERE: Pontefract town centre
COST: Most events are free
www.pontefractliquorice.co.uk

Learn how liquorice is made, stuff yourself silly, watch the parade and take part in the many games, crafts and activities for children and young people.

Tolpuddle Festival

WHEN: Mid July
WHERE: Tolpuddle, Dorset
COST: Free (entrance to festival and museum)
www.tolpuddlemartyrs.org.uk

This festival to celebrate the martyrs' trade union victory includes lots of activities for children: crafts, graffiti, football, storytelling and parachute games.

Sunderland International Airshow

WHEN: Late July
WHERE: Seaburn & Roker Seafront
COST: Free
www.sunderlandevents.co.uk

Europe's biggest free airshow. Impressive displays, entertainment and exhibitions galore.

Bristol Harbour Festival

WHEN: Late July
WHERE: Bristol Harbourside and locations throughout the city
COST: Free
www.bristolharbourfestival.co.uk

With its very own children's festival offering face painting, workshops, pirates and crafts, there's something for toddlers and teens at the Harbour Festival.

Festival of British Archaeology

WHEN: Mid July/early August
WHERE: Venues of historical/ archaeological importance throughout the UK
COST: Varies by event, some are free
www.britarch.ac.uk

Open excavations, hands-on activities for all the family, guided tours, exhibitions, lectures and lots more historical fun.

Sheringham Carnival

WHEN: Early August
WHERE: Sheringham, Norfolk
COST: Free or nominal entry to events
www.sheringhamcarnival.co.uk

Good old-fashioned seaside fun including a Strong Man competition, sandcastle building, fancy dress, a talent show, Bonny Baby competition and of course the carnival parade itself.

Liverpool Children's Festival

WHEN: Early August

WHERE: William Brown Street, Liverpool city centre

COST: Free

www.liverpoolchildrensfestival.org. uk

An arts and cultural event planned by children and young people for children and young people.

Kettlewell Scarecrow Festival

WHEN: Mid August

WHERE: Kettlewell

COST: Entry free, trail sheets for children are 50p

www.kettlewell.info

More than 100 homemade scarecrows mysteriously appear in gardens, shops and parks. Family trail with prizes.

England's Medieval Festival

WHEN: August Bank holiday weekend

WHERE: Herstmonceaux Castle, East Sussex

COST: Family £36, adults £17, children £10

www.englandsmedievalfestival.com

Archery, jousting, battle siege, falconry, medieval food and drink, medieval music, skill at arms and a kid's kingdom including face painting, juggling and wizardry.

Notting Hill Carnival Children's Day

WHEN: First day of the festival – late August

WHERE: Notting Hill, London

COST: Free

www.nottinghillcarnival.biz

Expect colourful parades, competitions, traditional Caribbean fun and games, music and young performers.

Bat Weekend

WHEN: Late August

WHERE: Events are held throughout the UK and Europe

COST: Mostly free

www.bats.org.uk,www.eurobats.org

See and hear bats in their natural environment by joining your local bat group in a guided dusk walk.

The Duxford Air Show

WHEN: Early September

WHERE: Imperial War Museum, Duxford, Cambridgeshire

COST: Adult £24.95, child £19.95, concessions apply

www.iwm.org.uk

Superb flying displays, the best of modern and historic aircraft, family-friendly fun and activities.

Bristol International Festival of Kites and Air Creations

WHEN: Early September

WHERE: Ashton Court Estate, Bristol

COST: Free entry

www.kite-festival.org

Amazing kite flying displays, kite-making workshops and lots of family fun.

National Mud Festival of Wales

WHEN: Early September

WHERE: National Wetlands Centre, Llanelli

COST: Free to WWT members, £7.30 adult, £4 child

www.wwt.org.uk

Mud, mud, glorious mud! Mud pies, mud competitions, arts, crafts and wildlife spotting.

London Freewheel

WHEN: Mid September
WHERE: Covers various routes through London
COST: Free
www.london.gov.uk/freewheel

An opportunity not to be missed! See the landmarks by cycling (children as well) through a car-free central London as traffic is stopped for the day. Organised rides available.

Bath Festival of Children's Literature

WHEN: Mid September
WHERE: Bath
COST: Varies by event, some are free
www.bathkidslitfest.co.uk

Join children's authors, illustrators, storytellers and poets for some literary family fun.

Bristol Open Doors Day

WHEN: Mid September
WHERE: Venues across Bristol including Bristol Old Vic
COST: Free
www.bristolopendoorday.org

A chance to see inside buildings of architectural or historical importance, many of which are not normally open to the public. Guided architectural tours and initiatives for young learners.

Open House London

WHEN: Mid September
WHERE: Venues in London including the Olympic site, Greenwich Peninsula and Royal Festival Hall
COST: Most events are £4.50, some are free

www.openhouse.org.uk

A chance to see inside buildings and sites of architectural or historical importance. Guided architectural tours and initiatives for young learners.

Open Rehearsal Weekend

WHEN: Late September
WHERE: Various theatres, museums and galleries throughout London and surrounding area
COST: Varies, much free
www.london.gov.uk/mayor/culture/open-rehearsal

From bell ringing to singing and dancing, to orchestral rehearsals and backstage theatre tours and workshops.

Tree Council Seed Gathering Season

WHEN: Late September – late October
WHERE: Locally organised events throughout the UK
COST: Free
www.treecouncil.org.uk

Join local conservationists in gathering seeds … and nurture the next generation of tree enthusiasts.

The Big Draw

WHEN: Early October
WHERE: East London and across the UK
COST: Most activities are free
www.campaignfordrawing.org

With more than 1,300 art and design style events across the UK for all ages. Get your kids drawing.

Red Squirrel Week

WHEN: Early October
WHERE: Various Wildlife Trust sites throughout the UK
COST: Most events are free
www.wildlifetrusts.org

See red with a week of conservation activities around our furry, lesser-known red squirrel friends.

Robin Hood Pageant

WHEN: Mid October
WHERE: Nottingham Castle
COST: Standard castle entry fees apply, £3 for adults (concessions apply). Free entry to Nottingham residents and workers
www.nottinghamcity.gov.uk

Jousting, real-ale, comic re-enactments, live music and a replica medieval village.

Family Learning Festival

WHEN: Mid October
WHERE: Venues around the UK
COST: Varies by event, some are free
www.welovelearning.co.uk

With more that 3,000 family events designed to make learning fun, this is the ideal place to kick start your brood's passion for learning!

National Schools Film Week

WHEN: Early-mid October
WHERE: Free screenings for school children at venues throughout London and the UK
COST: Free
www.nsfw.org

This series of special free screenings for children uses film as a medium to deliver complex information to a young audience in a meaningful way.

BBC Under 18 Electric Proms

WHEN: Mid October
WHERE: The Roundhouse, Camden
COST: Varies by event, some are free
www.roundhouse.org.uk

Workshops on everything from beatbox skills to sound engineering; a chance for 12 to 18 year olds to work on cutting-edge courses.

Wildscreen (biennial event)

WHEN: Mid October
WHERE: Watershed Media Centre, Bristol
COST: Varies by event
www.wildscreenfestival.org

Cannes for the wildlife documentary maker!

Apple Day

WHEN: Mid October
WHERE: Various UK locations including some National Trust properties
COST: Varies
www.commonground.co.uk/appleday

Bobbing, griggling, apple 'egg and spoon' races, apple printing, apple puppetry ... in fact, nearly all things apple.

Manchester Science Festival

WHEN: Late October
WHERE: Greater Manchester
COST: Varies by event, many are free
www.manchestersciencefestival.com

Lots of family friendly fun and explosive demonstrations to inspire the next generation of budding scientists.

RSPB Feed the Birds Day

WHEN: Mid/late October
WHERE: Various locations throughout the UK
COST: Free
www.rspb.org.uk/feedthebirds

Lots of family friendly fun including activities such as bird-cake making as well as expert advice on attracting and caring for birds.

Wildlife Photographer of the Year Exhibition

WHEN: Late October
WHERE: Natural History Museum, London (the exhibition also tours various other UK venues later in the year)
COST: Adults £7, children £3.50
www.nhm.ac.uk

Exhibition of winning photography with lots of kid-friendly initiatives to help budding photographers including a quiz, show and junior exhibition.

Juice Festival

WHEN: Late October – mid November
WHERE: Venues across Newcastle and Gateshead areas
COST: Varies by event, some events are free
www.newcastlegateshead.com

Celebrates creativity in children and young people. Take part in inspiring events, performances and activities with an artistic/literary bent.

London Children's Film Festival

WHEN: Mid November
WHERE: Barbican Centre, London
COST: Varies by event, some are free
www.londonchildrenfilm.org.uk

Films, workshops, events and 'hands-on film fun' including previews, premiers, world film, archive titles, shorts and sing-a-long favourites.

Glasgow Festival Radiance (biennial)

WHEN: Mid November
WHERE: Glasgow
COST: Free
www.seeglasgow.com/radiance

The International Festival of Light sees the transformation of famous buildings, bridges and graveyards using illumination.

The Bankside Frost Fair

WHEN: Mid December
WHERE: Bankside, Southward
COST: Free
www.visit.southwark.com

Enjoy ice-sculpture, carol singing, shopping, husky rides and lots of Christmassy make and do workshops.

Index

E

Easter
  bird's nest 205
  egg hunt 206
  piñata 207-208
eat
  out at home 45
  their words 49
  what you read 48
echo 133
elderflower cordial 51
elevenses *see* slow coffee
emergency kit 85
energy audit 139
England's Medieval Festival
    229
Exhibition Road Fete de la
    Musique 226
exotic fruits 56

F

family
  history 23
  picture tree 21-22
Family Learning Festival 231
farms
  grow your own 75
  pick-your-own 55
  wind 131
  worm 189
feather pen 36
Fierce Festival 225

fish in the city 163
flicker book 3
food
  in bedtime stories 48
  pretend 7
French breakfast 65
funeral for a toy 11
fungal foray 202
fungus wars 129

G

garden at the grandparents'
    house 74
gardens
  botanic 77
  create indoor 79
  grow in the kitchen 78
garlic 76
ginger beer 52-53
Glasgow Festival Radiance 232
Glastonbury Festival Kidz
    Field 226
Godzilla 116
gooey slime 134
Grand National Sheepstake
    224
gravity 137, 143
greyhounds 186
growing
  a farm 75
  a garden in the kitchen 78
  flowers and vegetables 69
  garlic 76

M

N

O

P

X

Notes

Acknowledgments

Thank you to all the writers whose work is featured in this book and also to Sharon Brooks, Rich Carr, Steve Chamberlain, Catherine Cronin, Lisa Darnell, Sara Montgomery, Polly Pattullo, Sally Weale and Laura Wheadon.